A BUBBLE THAT BROKE THE WORLD

GARET GARRETT

COSIMO CLASSICS

NEW YORK

TO

G. H. L.

*For his valiant doggedness and power
in moving the American thesis*

AUTHOR'S NOTE

Most of the matter in this book has appeared in the *Saturday Evening Post* during the last twelve months, though not exactly in the same form; and here the sequence is inverted, so that the view is from the present backward. Magazine articles that have been written to stand alone do not as a rule make a coherent whole for purposes of a book; on the other hand, pieces that were meant to be parts of a book may want that value of being current which a magazine article does like to possess. The merit of this arrangement, if any, is that you have a book of uncemented parts, any one of which may be taken by itself. Or take this to be a collected series of pamphlets, each of which is excited by certain phases of a subject that by reason somewhat of its own nature and somewhat of our ignorance about it is, in fact, formless.

G. G.

June 1, 1932

CONTENTS

A BUBBLE
THAT BROKE THE WORLD

COSMOLOGY OF THE BUBBLE

The Lord giveth increase, but man devised credit.

Mass delusions are not rare. They salt the human story. The hallucinatory types are well known; so also is the sudden variation called mania, generally localized, like the tulip mania in Holland many years ago or the common-stock mania of a recent time in Wall Street. But a delusion affecting the mentality of the entire world at one time was hitherto unknown. All our experience with it is original.

This is a delusion about credit. And whereas from the nature of credit it is to be expected that a certain line will divide the view between creditor and debtor, the irrational fact in this case is that for more than ten years debtors and creditors together have pursued the same deceptions. In many ways, as will appear, the folly of the lender has exceeded the extravagance of the borrower.

The general shape of this universal delusion may be indicated by three of its familiar features.

First, the idea that the panacea for debt is credit.

Debt in the present order of magnitude began with the World War. Without credit, the war could not have continued above four months; with benefit of credit it went more than four years. Victory followed the credit. The price was appalling debt. In Europe the war debt was both internal and external. The American war debt was internal only. This was the one country that borrowed nothing; not only did it borrow nothing, but parallel to its own war exertions it loaned to its European associates more than ten billions of dollars. This the European governments owed to the United States Treasury, besides what they owed to one another and to their own people. Europe's attack upon her debt, both internal and external, was a resort to credit. She called upon this country for immense sums of private credit—sums which before the war had been unimaginable—saying that unless American credit provided her with the ways and means to begin moving her burden of debt she would be unable to move it at all.

Result: The burden of Europe's private debt to this country now is greater than the burden of her war debt; and the war debt, with arrears of interest, is greater than it was the day the peace was signed. And it is not Europe alone. Debt was the economic terror of the world when the war ended. How to pay it was the colossal problem. Yet you will find hardly a nation, hardly any subdivision of a nation, state, city, town or region that has not multiplied its debt since the war. The aggregate of this increase is prodigious, and a very high proportion of it represents recourse to credit to avoid payment of debt.

Second, a social and political doctrine, now widely accepted, beginning with the premise that people are entitled to certain betterments of life. If they cannot immediately afford them, that is, if out of their own resources these betterments cannot be provided, nevertheless people are entitled to them, and credit must provide them. And lest it should sound unreasonable, the conclusion is annexed that if the standard of living be raised by credit, as of course it may be for a while, then people will be better creditors, better customers, better to live with and able at last to pay their debts willingly.

Result: Probably one half of all government, national and civic, in the area of western civilization is either bankrupt or in acute distress from having over-borrowed according to this doctrine. It has ruined the credit of countries that had no war debts to begin with, countries that were enormously enriched by the war trade, and countries that were created new out of the war. Now as credit fails and the standards of living tend to fall from the planes on which credit for a while sustained them, there is political dismay. You will hear that government itself is in jeopardy. How shall government avert social chaos, how shall it survive, without benefit of credit? How shall people live as they have learned to live, and as they are entitled to live, without benefit of credit? Shall they be told to go back? They will not go back. They will rise first. Thus rhetoric, indicating the emotional position. It does not say that what people are threatening to rise against is the payment of debt for credit devoured. When they have been living on credit beyond their means the debt overtakes them. If they tax themselves to pay it, that means going back a little. If they repudiate their debt, that is the end of their credit. In this dilemma the ideal solution, so recommended even to the creditor, is more credit, more debt.

Third, the argument that prosperity is a product of credit, whereas from the beginning of economic thought it had been supposed that prosperity was from the increase and exchange of wealth, and credit was its product.

This inverted way of thinking was fundamental. It rationalized the delusion as a whole. Its most astonishing imaginary success was in the field of international finance, where it became unorthodox to doubt that by use of credit in progressive magnitudes to inflate international trade the problem of international debt was solved. All debtor nations were going to meet their foreign obligations from a favorable balance of trade.

A nation's favorable balance in foreign trade is from selling more than it buys. Was it possible for nations to sell to one another more than they bought from one another, so that every one should have a favorable trade balance? Certainly. But how? By selling on credit. By lending one another the credit to buy one another's goods. All nations would not be able to lend equally, of course.

Each should lend according to its means. In that case this country would be the principal lender. And it was.

As American credit was loaned to European nations in amounts rising to more than a billion a year, in the general name of expanding our foreign trade, the question was sometimes asked: "Where is the profit in trade for the sake of which you must lend your customers the money to buy your goods?"

The answer was: "But unless we lend them the money to buy our goods they cannot buy them at all. Then what should we do with our surplus?"

As it appeared that European nations were using enormous sums of American credit to increase the power of their industrial equipment parallel to our own, all with intent to produce a great surplus of competitive goods to be sold in foreign trade, another question was sometimes asked: "Are we not lending American credit to increase Europe's exportable surplus of things similar to those of which we have ourselves an increasing surplus to sell? Is it not true that with American credit we are assisting our competitors to advance themselves against American goods in the markets of the world?"

The answer was: "Of course that is so. You must remember that these nations you speak of as competitors are to be regarded also as debtors. They owe us a great deal of money. Unless we lend them the credit to increase their power of surplus production for export they will never be able to pay us their debt."

Lingering doubts, if any, concerning the place at which a creditor nation might expect to come out, were resolved by an eminent German mind with its racial gift to subdue by logic all the difficult implication of a grand delusion. That was Doctor Schacht, formerly head of the German Reichsbank. He was speaking in this country. For creditor nations, principally this one, he reserved the business of lending credit through an international bank to the backward people of the world for the purpose of moving them to buy American radios and German dyes.

By this argument for endless world prosperity as a product of unlimited credit bestowed upon foreign trade, we loaned billions of American credit to our debtors, to our competitors, to our customers, with some beginning toward the backward people; we loaned credit to competitors who loaned it to their customers; we loaned credit to Germany who loaned credit to Russia for the purpose of enabling Russia to buy German things, including German chemicals. For several years there was ecstasy in the foreign trade. All the statistical curves representing world prosperity rose like serpents rampant.

Result: Much more debt. A world-wide collapse of foreign trade, by far the worst since the beginning of the modern epoch. Utter prostration of the statistical serpents. Credit representing many hundreds of millions of labor days locked up in idle industrial equipment both here and in Europe. It is idle because people cannot afford to buy its product at prices which will enable industry to pay interest on its debt. One country might forget its debt, set its equipment free, and flood the markets of the world with cheap goods, and by this offense kill off a lot of competition. But of course this thought occurs to all of them, and so all, with one impulse, raise very high tariff barriers against one another's goods, to keep them out. These tariff barriers may be regarded as instinctive reactions. They do probably portend a reorganization of foreign trade wherein the exchange of competitive goods will tend to fall as the exchange of goods unlike and noncompetitive tends to rise. Yet you will be almost persuaded that tariff barriers as such were the ruin of foreign trade, not credit inflation, not the absurdity of attempting by credit to create a total of international exports greater than the sum of international imports, so that every country should have a favorable balance out of which to pay its debts, but only this stupid way of people all wanting to sell without buying.

The life history of delusions, how they get born, grow up, grow old and die, would be an interesting study. The beginning and growth of this one may be easily traced. War, discovery and coincidence, all three, produced the occasion.

It took the war to discover in this country a power of production amazing to the world and no less to ourselves. We have forgotten how incredible it was. During the first few weeks of the war we were in a panic at the thought that to find money for their combat the nations of Europe might have to sell their holdings of American securities. If they were offered for sale on the New York Stock Exchange we should have to buy them.

Now, the total amount of Europe's holdings of American securities did not exceed five billions of dollars. Yet the prospect of having to repurchase five billions of American stocks and bonds from abroad was so terrifying that some of the elder international bankers in Wall Street proposed that this country should suspend gold payments. That is how little we knew of our own power. No one could have imagined that besides bailing our securities out of Europe, which we did on rising Stock Exchange quotations, we were about to spend twenty-five billions for participation in Europe's war and lend our European associates more than ten billions at the same time—all in less than five years. To the world at large this was like the discovery of an infinitely rich new continent upon the explored earth; to us it was an astounding self-revelation.

The coincidence was that after many years of blundering toward it, and only a few months before the beginning of the war in Europe, we had found the formula for the most efficient credit machine that was ever invented. This was the Federal Reserve System. The law creating it was enacted in December, 1913. The extraordinary merit of the idea was that it contemplated for the first time a flexible currency to expand and con·

tract in rhythm with the demands of trade and industry. Business to generate its own finance. That was the idea, and it worked. But as it worked that way, the credit resources of the old underlying national bank system and of the forty-eight separate state banking systems, hitherto employed to finance business through its seasons and cycles, were very largely released for other purposes, whatever they might be. Purposes of investment, promotion and speculation.

The new order arrived just in time. Without it we should not have been able so easily to receive our securities back from Europe, nor to finance the war trade, nor to make those early private loans to the combatant nations. An Anglo-French loan for $500,000,000 was the first notable test of its strength. And no sooner was it tried and found answerable in hundreds of millions than it had to be tested in tens of billions to finance the war loans of the United States Government, borrowing both for itself and our European associates at the same time.

When the war was over this country was paramount in two dimensions. Its industrial power was apparently limitless and it had the finest credit machine in the world. Certainly these ingredients were potent; and the road was strange.

It had long been the darling theme of a few world minds among us that as a people we should learn to "think internationally." We never had. Then suddenly we found ourselves in the leading international part, cast there by circumstances, with no experience, no policy rationally evolved, no way of thinking about it. To "think internationally", if it had ever been defined, was a way of thinking not of ourselves alone, but of others too, as all belonging to one world. In our anxiety to overtake this idea we overran it; international-mindedness became a way of thinking not of ourselves first but of the world first, of the other people in it, and of our responsibilities to them. No nation ever did think that way. If a nation did it would not long endure. To suppose this nation in its right mind could or would was the first sign of the oncoming delusion.

A variety of influences, incongruous among themselves, ran together to bring it on. There was the sentimental influence first. For nearly two years after the armistice the American Government continued making loans to European countries for their general relief, extending them even to the side that was enemy, and did this with unlimited popular sanction. At the same time private assistance was offered and received on sentimental grounds. Societies were formed to adopt European towns and villages. The recovery of Europe was much more than our economic concern; we made it our emotional anxiety. Internationalism as a political cult seized the occasion to press its propaganda upon a receptive national mind. Friends of Europe organized themselves into eminent groups to support the European thesis for war debt cancellation at the expense of the American taxpayer. The direct influence of Europe was very powerful. In developing the thought of our unlimited moral and economic responsibility for the rehabilitation of Europe there was but one Old World voice; it spoke continually in all European languages, thus preparing, whether consciously or not, a fabulous source of credit. And at last American finance, as might have been foretold, went international, with a body of highly accented doctrine, some of it quite unsound, yet very appealing to the self-interest of American agriculture and American industry, both in a nightmare of surplus and easily persuaded that the only solution was in foreign trade, bought with American credit.

Neither agriculture nor industry cared how it was bought, only so long as some one else seemed to be paying for it. In the end everybody paid for it. The loss that fell upon the private investor fell also upon the whole country. Those foreign outlets for the surplus we were so anxious to get rid of turned out to be very costly.

To say there was no way with our surplus but to lend it away is simply to say that at this time our imagination failed. We kept thinking of surplus credit, and there is no such thing, short of total human satiety. That we had power to produce more food than we could eat ourselves, or more automobiles than we could use ourselves, was not a sign of surplus except in a particular, unimaginative sense. The power of production is in itself infinitely versatile. If there is more of it than we need to satisfy our immediate wants, then instead of using it to produce a surplus of goods to lend away in the foreign trade we may use it to perform prodigious collective works for the future. Or by economic and financial engineering we may convert it into credit and conserve it, as wild water is conserved, behind dams, against a time of famine. One way to convert and store it would be to pay off the public debt so that to meet any emergency thereafter the government should have a free, tremendous borrowing power, with no worry about its budget. But all the time it was easier to let it run away in happy torrents.

Obsessed with the thought of having a surplus of goods and a surplus of credit that we were obliged to lend, only to be rid of them, still there was no surplus in this country of good housing for people of low income in the cities. There was and is enormous need for such housing. The credit with which to meet it is difficult to command. Yet American credit was loaned freely to other countries for that purpose, notably to Germany. Capital borrowed on public credit to replace slum dwellings with model tenements may not be very profitable. It seldom is. But if we use our own capital for that purpose, even though it be lost, still we have the model tenements. If we build pyramids with our own credit at least we have the pyramids to enjoy; if we use our credit for works of private profit that turn out badly, the creditors who loaned the credit may send the sheriff to sell the property into new hands for what it will bring, and although we

have wasted some credit, we have the externalized cor-
porality of it entire.

But if we lend our credit to foreign countries and they
build pyramids with it, we have to spend money in foreign
travel even to look at them; and if we lend our credit for
skyscrapers and railroads and power plants to be built in
foreign countries and these turn out badly we cannot
send the sheriff to seize them. Where is the State of
Minas Geraes? You would not be expected to know. We
loaned sixteen millions of American credit to the State
of Minas Geraes, and all we know about it is that the
bonds of Minas Geraes are in default. If Amarillo, Texas,
had lost sixteen millions of American credit we should
at least know where to go to look for it.

It is true that while what we called surplus American
credit was vanishing abroad in sums rising to two billions
a year, going to places we had never heard of and for
purposes that sometimes were not even stated, public
borrowing in the United States also was extravagant.
Many cities and States were borrowing perhaps more
than they could afford. Private borrowing in the United
States at the same time may have been as reckless as
private borrowing anywhere else. Say it was. There is
still the difference between knowing and not knowing
your debtor; between knowing and not knowing what
he did with it, between the right of the creditor in his own
country to lay hands on the property and his inability
to act upon the news that his Brazilian bond is in default.
He will receive the news by a printed form from the
same American banking house that sold the bonds, now
acting as Brazil's fiscal agent. Of the many Brazilian
bonds floated in this country he may happen to have one
of the issue named in the banker's prospectus: "$25,000,-
000 United States of Brazil (Central Railway Electrifica-
tion Loan of 1922) 30-year 7 per cent. Gold Bonds."
The bonds are in default and the Central Railway was
never electrified. What was done with the credit only

Brazil knows. The bankers do not know. And what can be done about it is nothing.

The holder of a foreign bond must have bought it on faith. There was no other way. How could the individual investor examine for himself the economic resources of a foreign country and analyze its budget, or enter into the private accounts of a foreign corporation, try its balance sheet, and form a judgment, besides, of its prospects in the field?

On the science, wonder and romance of American investments abroad, on the individual investor's perilous position in faith and on the moral responsibility of the banker, a very beautiful essay was written by the late Dwight W. Morrow, who had been a member of the house of J. P. Morgan and Company, international bankers; then Ambassador to Mexico, later United States Senator. It was printed in *Foreign Affairs,* an American quarterly of international vision, in the year 1927 (a year in which our loans to foreign countries exceeded the total borrowing of all American States, counties, townships, districts, towns, boroughs and cities). This essay became at once a classic of the kind, referred to continually by all who wanted a theory or a philosophy of what we were doing. He was on a train, reading a Chicago newspaper, and he counted the foreign bonds listed in its daily bond table. The number was 128, where ten years before, as he learned by inquiry, there had been only six. He wrote:

"Examining that long list of 128 bonds I discovered that governments, municipalities or corporations of some 30 different countries were represented—countries scattered all over the world. The list included the countries of our own hemisphere, Canada, Cuba, Brazil, Argentina, Chile, Peru, Bolivia, Uruguay; nations abroad with whom we fought and against whom we fought; governments in the Far East such as Japan and the Dutch East Indies; and cities as widely separated as Copenhagen and Montevideo, Tokio and Marseilles.

"The contemplation of the extent and variety of America's investments in foreign bonds gives rise to three questions: Who buys these bonds? Why do they buy them? What do they get when they have bought them?"

These questions he set himself to answer. From statistical evidence he concluded that more than four buyers in every five were small investors and bought them in amounts from $100 up to $5,000. On this he said: "The investment in these foreign loans represents the savings of the person who spends less than he produces and thus creates a fund which he is able to turn over either to a domestic or to a foreign borrower. . . . When we talk about the person who is investing in foreign bonds we are not talking about a great institution in New York or Chicago or Boston. We are talking about thousands of people living in all parts of the United States. We are talking about schoolteachers and army officers and country doctors and stenographers and clerks."

Then the second question: Why do they buy foreign bonds? "Here," he wrote, "statistics are of little value. . . . The considerations in the minds of most investors are, first, the safety of the principal, and, second, the size of the interest yield. It should be borne in mind that the investor is the man who has done without something. He has done without something that he might presently have enjoyed in order that, in the future, his family may have some protection when he is gone, or in order, perhaps, that a son or a daughter may go to college. This investor wants to be certain that he will continue to receive income on the bond which he buys. He wants that income as large as is consistent with safety. Above all, he wants the principal returned to him on the day of the maturity of the bond. It cannot be asserted, however, that sentiment plays no part in our investments. It does. Many men in this country bought German bonds, after the successful launching of the Dawes Plan, not only because the rate of interest was attractive and the principal seemed secure, but because they felt that they were thus associating themselves in a fine venture to help Europe back on her feet." Sentiment allowed its due weight, yet Mr. Morrow supposed safety was always the first consideration. And he asked: "If that be true, how is the investor to form an intelligent judgment as to the safety of his investment? If he should be asked this question, I think that he would put in the very forefront of his reasons for making the investment the fact that he had confidence in the banker who offered him the investment. This throws a heavy responsibility upon the banker."

Thirdly, the question: What does the buyer of a foreign bond get? On that he continued: "In 1924, 40 persons in a western city put $100 apiece into a Japanese bond maturing in 1954. What did those people get for their money? They got a promise. And, mark you, that promise was the promise of a group of people associated together on the other side of the earth. Moreover, so far as the promise relates to the payment of the principal of the bond, the promise does not mature in time to be kept by the particular members of the group who originally made it. It is a promise designed to be kept by the children of men now living. Yet somehow or other, the banker who offers that bond and the investor who buys that bond rely on the people of Japan taxing themselves a generation from now in order to pay back the principal of that bond to the children of the person who invests in the bonds today. At first blush it is a startling idea. It is particularly startling at this time when so many people are saying that the various nations of the earth have lost faith in each other. Here we have printed in a middle western newspaper the record of the day's dealings in 128 foreign bond issues. Individuals in America are taking their own money, with its present command over goods and services, and surrendering that command to nations on the other side of the earth, and they receive in exchange for it a promise. The question may be asked: Nothing more than a promise? To which the answer may be made: Nothing less than a promise. . . . Those nations who are borrowing in America because they actually need the money for a constructive purpose, who have a solidarity of national feeling and a sense of the meaning and value of national credit, who are not incurring obligations beyond what may fairly be considered their capacity to handle them— all those nations may be expected to pay their debts. Here again the responsibility rests heavily upon the investment banker recommending investments. The banker must never be lured, either by the desire for profit or the desire for reputation, to recommend an investment which he does not believe to be good."

Two years later the crystal burst. Within four years the loss upon American investments abroad was incalculable. Of the new Latin-American bond issues that had been recommended to investors by the very best Wall Street banks and their bond-selling affiliates—of these alone, fifty-six issues, aggregating more than eight hundred millions of dollars, were in default; and the fate of others not actually in default was very uncertain. In Europe, with a general moratorium on war debts and reparations, with a private moratorium running to Germany, another one to Austria, another one to Hungary, and with war debts and private debts involved in one great maelstrom of political controversy, the value of the American investment, present or ultimate, was very indefinite. Bonds of the German Government selling on the New York Stock Exchange at thirty to sixty cents on the dollar, bonds of the State of Prussia at twenty-five cents, bonds of the City of Berlin at twenty cents, Hungarian bonds at fifteen to forty cents, many of the private bonds of European industry a little better or a little worse; and these were all bonds that had been eminently sold to the American investor within five or six years at ninety, ninety-five and one hundred. Then one by one the international bankers appeared before committees of inquiry of the United States Senate, all saying they thought the bonds were good and all alike disavowing further responsibility. They had not guaranteed the bonds or the validity of them. They were not responsible for how the money was spent or misspent; the borrowers were responsible. And as for the _foreign bond delirium_ in this country, that was something the people, that is to say, the private investors, had done to themselves.

Before the Committee on Finance of the United States Senate, the head of the second largest national bank in Wall Street, who represented also the most aggressive bond-selling organization in the world, appeared and said: "We are merchants. With respect to bonds generally, we are merchants."

A member of the most powerful private international banking house said to the same committee: "We are merchants. That is what we are, just like any merchant, in the grain business, in the cotton business, or anything else."

The head of the largest national bank in Wall Street, one that owns also a very powerful bond-selling organization, appeared before the Senate Committee on Manufactures. The committee was hearing bankers on the question of establishing a national economic council and it was asking him what the bankers had done to restrain a wild use of American credit before the collapse. He said: "Speculation was in the air, and the speculators wanted to buy, buy, buy, and the bankers and brokers dealing in securities supplied that demand. . . . In other words, I do not think you would be justified in holding the bankers responsible for the wide speculative craze that worked through the country. I think they were trying to supply what the customers wanted. . . . I think the banker is like the grocer. He supplies what his customer wants."

And to that committee the head again of the second largest national bank in Wall Street, who appeared twice in Washington—looking at the same subject, namely, the delirious use of American credit in foreign securities—said: "It came about in part by reason of the public's interest in, and fever and fervor for, investments and speculation, if you will. It came about as a result of the demands of foreign countries for funds and an obvious appetite on the part of the American public for investments therein. The investment banking community became one of the tools by which the demands on each side operated to satisfy their requirements."

Grocers, merchants and automatic tools. And the people Mr. Morrow wrote about all did it to themselves. Their sudden appetite for foreign bonds was so voracious that if they had read in every case the banker's prospectus, which few of them did, they perhaps would not have noticed the line in smaller type that always appeared at the bottom and read: "The information contained in this circular has been obtained partly from cable and other official sources. While not guaranteed, it is accepted by us as accurate."

Not even the accuracy of the information was guaranteed by the banker.

The Senate Committee on Finance learned a good deal about the merchant banker trade. It learned how foreign bonds originate in Wall Street and how they get from there to the hands of the individual investor. As in trade generally, there are parts, three at least and sometimes four, corresponding to the parts, respectively, of manufacturer, jobber, wholesaler, retailer.

There is first the bank that discovers and originates the bond issue. Let the borrower be a foreign government. The bank undertakes to buy from the foreign government so many bonds of a certain character at 90, and to pay for them on maybe the tenth day following the public offering. This originating bank then calls in a jobbing group of two or three banks of its own rank and says to them: "Here is a good thing. We will share it with you at 90½." So the jobbing group underwrites the bond issue at 90½, which is the first step-up. The jobbing group then forms a large syndicate of wholesalers, to whom it will sell the bonds at 92. This is the second step-up. The wholesalers know the retail trade; that is their business. Each wholesaler has a card index of retail bond dealers all over the country, with notations indicating about how many bonds of a certain kind each retailer may be expected to sell to the banks in his neighborhood and to the individual investors in his community. The wholesalers, by letter, telephone and telegraph, offer this new bond to the retail trade at 94, which is the third step-up, and the retailers will sell them to the public at 96½, so that the retailer's profit will be 2½ per cent., which is the last step-up.

When all these arrangements are made, the jobbing group advertises the bonds in the newspapers and at the same time establishes on the curb market, or over the bank counters, a public quotation a fraction above the retail price, say, 96⅝. This is the public offering. The originating house delivers the bonds to the jobbers, who deliver them to the wholesalers, who scatter them widely to the retail trade, and that day thousands of bond salesmen begin to solicit the small-town bank presidents and all the people Mr. Morrow wrote about, to buy the bonds. As the bonds are sold, the money starts moving from the many local sources toward Wall Street. Ten days after the public offering the wholesalers settle with the jobbers and the jobbers settle with the originating house and the foreign government gets its money. There are variations of the price steps, and, if the bond issue is small and juicy, the jobbers may go direct to the retail trade or the wholesalers themselves may perform the jobbing function, so that there may be only three steps instead of four; but with such slight modifications, the method as described is standard.

The only risk the Wall Street banker takes, you see, is

in judging the public appetite. If his judgment is good the
bonds are sold and paid for before the foreign government
gets the money. The desirability of that result explains
the speed and high tension at which all the machinery
works.

All of that the committee could understand. Given the
point of view of the international banker, that he is like a
grocer, and then the uncontrollable demand on the part
of the American public for his merchandise, it could
understand why representatives of Wall Street banking
houses went frantically to and fro in the world, pressing
American credit upon foreign governments, foreign cities,
foreign corporations, soliciting them to issue bonds to
satisfy that American appetite; why at one time twenty-
nine such representatives were all soliciting a small Latin-
American country to make a bond issue in Wall Street;
even why American bankers paid large commissions, vul-
garly mentioned as bribes, to influential private persons
in foreign countries who could lead them to a new bond
issue. It received with pleasure an acknowledgment of
practical error from the head of a private banking house
who said: "Yes, but it is also true that those things
existed not only in Latin America, but the world over,
relating to governments, municipalities and industrial
concerns. In other words, the accumulation of capital in
America was seeking an outlet, The bankers were the
instruments of the outlet. They were the purveyors of
capital. The bankers competed to a degree that in retro-
spect was wholly wrong. I am not speaking morally."

And yet all the simplicity of light that could be brought
to bear upon these points seemed only more and more to
obscure one another. The committee became very uneasy
about it. Given again that inebriate demand on the part
of the American investor which obliged the merchant
banker to search the world for foreign borrowers, why
then was it necessary for the bankers to adopt the intensive
merchandising methods of industry in order to dispose of

their merchandise? One would suppose it had sold itself, even faster than it could be originated. Why were foreign bonds so expensively advertised? Why were they pressed upon the investor through costly, he-type selling organizations, by house-to-house canvass, even in some cases by radio ballyhoo? Questions to this point seemed always to embarrass the banker witnesses. The least indefinite answer either of the Senate committees got was made by the head of the foremost banking organization in Wall Street. He said: "Oh, undoubtedly salesmanship and advertising facilitate business; but you must remember that the banker cannot make that profit from his advertising and salesmanship unless the market is there to sell on, and unless the public is there to buy."

One point was too clear. There was no American policy. First and last, exclusive of the loans by United States Government to its European war associates, private American credit to the incredible aggregate, roughly, of fifteen billions was loaned in foreign countries—without a policy.

If the State Department did touch foreign loans, it was with an ambiguous finger. Only once was the government openly positive, and that is how the State Department's contact with foreign loans began. When the United States Treasury stopped making post-armistice loans direct to European countries they all turned to Wall Street and began there to borrow private credit very heavily, while at the same time they were refusing to go to the United States Treasury and fund their promissory war-time notes into long-term bonds, according to the terms of their war loan contracts. So the government declared that it would disapprove of private American loans to foreign countries that were unwilling to honor their obligations to the United States Treasury. The government could not forbid their borrowing in Wall Street; it could only express its disapproval. But that was enough. All the debtor nations then came and did with their war debts at the United States Treasury what they had agreed to do.

Out of this arose the practice, which still continues, of referring a foreign loan to the State Department before it is publicly offered, to see if the government has any political objection to it. If there is none, the State Department says so and the bond issue proceeds; but what the State Department says is negative only, and confidential. When the State Department says there is no political objection to a foreign loan it does not thereby approve of the loan, or assume any moral responsibility whatever. The bankers understand this. Nevertheless, as it became generally known that all foreign bond issues were first referred to the State Department, the idea somehow grew up in the popular mind that they were issued under the sanction of the State Department, which was never so.

By informality the government did effectively object to a loan Wall Street would have floated for the Franco-German potash monopoly. The reasons were obvious to all but the bankers. Before the war this had been a Prussian monopoly. The whole world was dependent upon Germany for an indispensable plant food, a fact which entered deeply into the calculations of the German militarists as to how they should run the world after the German victory. But after the war France had the potash beds of Alsace, by cession of Alsace-Lorraine, whereupon the French and Germans agreed to handle potash as a joint monopoly and divided between them the markets of the world. During the war potash in this country went from $40 to $400 a ton because we were cut off from the German supply and our soil was starving for it. Only ten years later and with American chemical science struggling to develop American sources of potash as a vital national possession, Wall Street, but for the objection of the government, would have loaned $25,000,000 of American credit to strengthen the Franco-German monopoly.

The enormous German borrowing in Wall Street, after the Dawes Plan loan, was a source of constant anxiety to the government, as it was to all observers whose motives were free and whose minds had not been seized by delusion. There was the danger, first, that if Germany's external private debts went on growing they would come into conflict with her reparation debts to France, Great Britain, Belgium, and others, as at last they did; and the danger, moreover, that such extravagant borrowing would bring Germany's whole financial structure to insolvency, as it did. Yet apparently there was nothing that could stop it.

S. Parker Gilbert, the American Agent General for Reparation Payments, under the Dawes Plan, addressed a public protest to the German Government, which he concluded by saying: "I have attempted to bring together in the foregoing pages the accumulating evidences of overspending and overborrowing on the part of the German public authorities, and some of the indications of artificial stimulation and overexpansion that are already manifesting themselves. These tendencies, if allowed to continue unchecked, are almost certain, on the one hand, to lead to severe economic reaction and depression, and are likely, on the other hand, to encourage the impression that Germany is not acting with due regard to her reparation obligations."

That made no difference. Wall Street ignored the warning. Again, writing from Paris to American bankers, November 3, 1926, Mr. Gilbert said: "I am constantly amazed at the recklessness of American bankers in offering to the public the securities of German States on the basis of the purely German view of Article 248 of the Treaty of Versailles. It is a simple matter, of course, to get letters from the financial authorities of the German States setting forth the German point of view, and I can easily understand the willingness of the German authorities to sign letters stating the German point of view, but it does seem to me difficult to justify the action of the American bankers in offering the securities to the public on the basis of such letters, without giving the slightest hint that the

German point of view is not accepted by the Allied governments, and that, in fact, the Allied point of view is diametrically opposed."

Sir William Leese, of the Bank of England, supported Mr. Gilbert with an analysis of the representations being made to American investors in respect of two important German loans, and stated the following conclusion: "Upon this point both prospectuses are in my opinion substantially untrue and misleading." One for the City of Hamburg and one for the State of Prussia.

And that made no difference. The State Department, though not objecting to any particular German loan, addressed a letter to the issuing houses in Wall Street, saying: ". . . It cannot be said at this time that serious complications in connection with interest and amortization payments by German borrowers may not arise from possible future action by the agent general and the transfer committee. . . . A further point which the department feels should be considered by you . . . is the provision of Article 248 of the Treaty of Versailles, under which 'a first charge upon all the assets and revenues of the German Empire and its constituent States' is created in favor of reparation and other treaty payments. . . . These risks, which obviously concern the investing public, should in the opinion of the department be cleared up by you before any action is taken. If they cannot be definitely eliminated, the department believes that you should consider whether you do not owe a duty to your prospective clients fully to advise them of the situation."

But so long as the government did not positively object, Wall Street went on bringing out German bond issues, faster and faster—the bonds of German States, German cities, German regions, German industry, German agriculture, German ports, anything German. Moreover, it kept hundreds of representatives in Germany soliciting all of these sources for bonds to sell to the American public.

In much of our lending to Europe, particularly as it

ran to Germany, there was a sense of gesture. American credit was the rich prodigal returning in a grand way from a far country to dazzle and reward the indigent ancestor. And whether it was that some of the sentiment discovered by Mr. Morrow in his small investors worked itself up to the Wall Street mind, or that Wall Street itself needed emotional reasons and naturally acquired them, the fact is that bankers themselves became assertively sentimental about Germany. It is true that thinking of the effect of reparation payments upon the new German debt they were creating here might have inclined them realistically to the well-known German view of reparations; but they went much further and considered the effect of reparations upon the hearts and minds of Germans born since the war and of Germans yet unborn.

This was discovered to the Senate Committee on Finance by one of its most eminent banker witnesses, who said: "Here we have in Germany to-day young men going into the universities of Germany who were not born when the great war started. Those young men see that not only must they pay, but their progeny and the progeny of their progeny, must pay, and go on for these generations in paying a debt for which they, as individuals, were not responsible. They feel that they are under a heavy yoke, and my impression is that there is growing, as a result thereof, rebellion against payment of the debt."

Senator Reed asked this startling question: "Why should the progeny of Americans who had nothing to do with the war, the progeny of Americans who were not even alive, pay this war debt, and the progeny of the people who started it go scot free?"

The banker answered: "I grant you that that is quite unanswerable as an argument within itself."

If at any time you had asked an international banker to say whether or not there was an American policy to govern foreign loans he would have said yes, and if you had asked what it was, he would have said: "More and more our prosperity is and will be dependent on foreign trade. American loans abroad represent an investment in foreign trade."

This is not a policy. It is an idea only, largely fallacious as such. Here we have no state policy, as in France, that stipulates for political and economic advantages in return for credit loaned in other countries; nor is there here, as in England, the organized practice of tying up foreign loans with foreign contracts. American credit is loaned on the obscure presumption that trade will somehow follow; the borrowers, having got the credit, may do with it what they like.

Moreover, wherein our foreign loans do increase American exports, who is it that takes thought beforehand of how payment shall be received? Suppose the debtor offers to make payment in competitive goods that we do not want, and says he cannot pay in any other measure. That is happening. It is what is bound to happen when we lend American credit to foreign countries to increase their production of competitive goods; and the problem then is how we shall receive payment at all, if we keep a tariff against the exportable goods of our debtors.

But even that idea of buying foreign trade with American credit, to make outlets for the American surplus, was not consistently pursued. Take some typical instances.

With the American Government borrowing credit to lend at low rates of interest to people who will build ships, thereby to foster an American merchant marine, American credit is loaned in large sums to German shipping companies; they use it to build German ships in German shipyards, with German labor and German materials, to compete with American ships.

With American chemical science dimly in sight of its goal, which is to make this country independent of Germany's synthetic chemistry, American credit is loaned to the German Dye Trust, whereby its offensive powers, in trade or in war, are strengthened.

If these are not cases in which we could not afford to lend American credit on any terms, still, where was the benefit to our own foreign trade? Lending very large sums of American credit to the Anglo-Chilean Nitrate Trust does neither increase the volume of American exports nor foreshorten the time in which we may hope by synthetic chemistry to free ourselves from dependence upon foreign sources of nitrogenous fertilizers and the essential chemical products of nitrate; and the same is to be said of loans of American credit to German and Italian corporations for the purpose of building nitrogen fixation plants. Lending forty million dollars of American credit to a foreign oil company, for drilling and exploration, can hardly be called an investment in our own foreign trade, nor a loan of one hundred and fifty million dollars of American credit to the Dutch East Indies to pay off its floating debt. It would be difficult to explain how lending large sums of American credit to the fabulous Swedish Match Trust, which in turn made loans to European governments in exchange for monopolistic trade concessions, benefited the sale of American goods in the foreign trade. Certainly a loan of American credit to a Latin-American republic to pay a debt it owed in Europe for armament had no beneficial trace in the American foreign trade. Or fancy any benefit to the American export trade from a loan of twenty millions to a German bank for the specific purpose, as stated by the bankers, "to finance German exporting corporations."

Glance at the contradiction of lending very large sums of American credit for the purpose of extending, improving and financing Europe's agriculture, with the American Government borrowing credit to support the price of American wheat because the European demand for American grain declined. The word for this may be one of unction or it may be cynical, from opposite points of view, but certainly there was no policy in it. If for any reason we were going to lend our credit to extend

Europe's agriculture, we should have been providing at the same time both the credit and the economic engineering to shrink American agriculture proportionately, without disaster to the farmer.

Loans to Europe, especially to Germany, to rationalize industry and introduce American methods of mass production could benefit American industry in the foreign trade only if you argued that what American industry needed for its own good was more competition.

But of all the ways in which the lending of American credit in Europe did not increase the American export trade, the one most extraordinary was that of lending our debtors the credit with which to make payment to us on their debt. American loans to Germany enabled Germany to pay reparations to the Allies; reparations from Germany enabled the Allies to pay interest on their war debts at the United States Treasury, hardly touching their own pockets. We were paying ourselves. For a long time this simple construction was denied and concealed in the elaborate confusions of finance. The Senate Committee on Finance kept asking its banker witnesses to face it. One of the best answers was by Otto H. Kahn, who said:

"There is no doubt that if Germany had not been able to borrow money it would have been unable, long since, to pay reparations, and, therefore, to that extent, it is a generally correct statement to say that out of the money which Germany borrowed it did pay reparations."

Then at last the German Government itself, to prove Germany's incapacity to pay, publicly declared that reparations had been paid only by borrowing and that if Germany could not continue to borrow she could not continue to pay.

That debt need never be paid, that it may be infinitely postponed, that a creditor nation may pay itself by progressively increasing the debts of its debtors—such was the logic of this credit delusion.

Since John Law and his Mississippi Bubble, individuals have been continually appearing with the same scheme in new disguise. The principle is very simple. You have only to find a way to multiply your creditors by the cube and pay them by the square, out of their own money. Then for a while you are Nabob. One fish cut up for bait brings three. Two of these cut up for bait bring eight, the cube of two. Four of these cut up for bait bring sixty-four, the cube of four. Sixteen of these for bait bring 4,096, and 256 of these, which is the square of sixteen, will bring 16,777,216, which is the cube of 256.

The fatal weakness of the scheme is that you cannot stop. When new creditors fail to present themselves faster than the old creditors demand to be paid off, the bubble bursts. Then you go to jail, like Ponzi, or commit suicide, like Ivar Kreuger.

There is nothing new in the scheme. What is new is that for the first time the whole world tried it. The whole world cannot put itself in jail, nor can it escape the consequences by suicide.

When the delusion breaks, people all with one impulse hoard their money, banks all with one impulse hoard credit, and debt becomes debt again, as it always was. Credit is ruined. Suddenly there is not enough for everyday purposes. Yet only a little while before we had been saying and thinking there was a great surplus of American credit and the only thing we could do with it was to export it. How absurd it sounds in echo. It was absurd at the time.

Our problem properly was, properly is, for a long time will be, how to find enough credit to perform the works that lie ahead of us, only such as are in sight. We already see that we shall have to recast the entire transportation machine, wherein is to be faced both a terrific loss of old capital and the necessity to provide in place of it enormous sums of new capital. We already know that we shall have to relate and organize in a rational manner our sources of energy by bringing the three hydrocarbons, coal, gas and oil, into a few immense pools, where they may be converted interchangeably into forms ideal for the several needs of life, industry and commerce, and whence they may be distributed, without waste, more and more efficiently, until fuel, heat, light and power shall become as cheap as water. We have our cities to make over, not to meet their future, but only to accommodate the change that has already occurred in the patterns and conditions of American life. There is no suburban area but must be reclaimed from its anarchy of free growth and recast to a regional plan by colossal engineering.

The new materials and methods discovered almost daily by science are creating obsolescence at a rate never before imagined. Notwithstanding the physical progress everywhere to show, the fact is that in contrast with the present state of technical and scientific knowledge and the power we possess, the country is more in arrears than it was a generation ago; it has much more to overtake. Many of the blue prints are ready and fading for want of credit.

ANATOMY OF THE BUBBLE

Who, then, is he who provides it all? Go and find him and you will have once more before you The Forgotten Man. . . . The Forgotten Man is delving away in patient industry, supporting his family, paying his taxes, casting his vote, supporting the church and the school, reading his newspaper, and cheering for the politician of his admiration, but he is the only one for whom there is no provision in the great scramble and the big divide.

—WILLIAM GRAHAM SUMNER

Command of labor and materials built the pyramids. The economic world was then very simple. Some private usury, of course, but no banking system, no science of credit, no engraved securities issued on the pyramids for investors to worry about. Merely, the whim of Pharaoh, his idea of a pyramid, his power to move labor, and the fact of a surplus of food enough to sustain those who were diverted from agriculture to monumental masonry.

It is believed that on Cheops alone 100,000 men were employed for twenty years. And when it was finished all that Egypt had to show for 600,000,000 days of human labor was a frozen asset. Otherwise and usefully employed, as, for example, upon habitations and hearthstones, works of common utility, means of national defense, that amount of labor might have raised the standard of common living in Egypt to a much higher plane, besides insuring Egyptian civilization a longer competitive life. But once it had been spent on a pyramid to immortalize the name of Pharaoh it was spent forever. People could not consume what their own labor had produced. That is to say, they could not eat a pyramid, or wear it, or live in it, or make any use of it whatever. Not even Pharaoh could sell it, rent it, or liquidate it.

History does not say what happened to the 100,000 when Cheops was finished. Were they unemployed? Were they returned to agriculture whence they came? If so, that would be like now sending suddenly four or five million people from industry back to the farms in this country.

You may take it, at any rate, that when Cheops was finished, there occurred in Egypt what we should call an economic crisis, with no frightful statistics, no collapsing index numbers in the daily papers, no stock-exchange panic, no bank failures, but with unemployment, blind social turmoil, Egyptian bread lines perhaps. And this crisis, like every crisis since, down to the very last, was absorbed by people who could not consume what they had produced, whose labor had been devoured by a pile of stones, and who understood it dimly if at all. The forgotten people.

This story of a pyramid has the continuing verity of a parable. For all the worlds that have passed since that Egyptian civilization departed, for all the new wonders of form, method and power that seem to make this one of ours original, nevertheless, what happened to the forgotten people of Egypt happens still in our scheme; it happens to The Forgotten Man of William G. Sumner's classic essay, and for the same reasons.

There is here no solitary Pharaoh with the power to move labor by word alone. In this world labor is free, receiving wages. Yet you have to see that the passion among us for individual and collective aggrandizement by command of labor and materials is what it always was and that the consequences of pursuing it far in selfish and uneconomic ways are what they are bound to be and anciently were.

In place of one responsible Pharaoh at a time, we have a multitude of irresponsible Pharaohs; and beyond these we have the Pharaoh passion acting in governments big and little, in States and cities, in great private and public organizations, all seeking their own exaggeration and all seeking it by the one means. The motive may be avarice, it may be good or bad, it may derive from a sense of rivalry between nations or from an idea of public happiness. In the nature of economic consequences, strange to say, the motive does not matter. A pyramid is a pyramid still. When too much labor has been spent upon pyramids, or things that are unproductive and dead in the economic meaning of pyramids, there will be a crisis in daily wellbeing, and free labor in that case will be as helpless as slave labor was. It cannot consume what it has produced; it is without all those human satisfactions that might have been produced with the same labor in place of the pyramid, and it is without them forever. The labor that is lost cannot be recovered by unbuilding the pyramid.

But in this world where labor is free and no one has the apparent power to move it beyond its own volition, how is it moved or procured to waste itself too far upon works of public and private aggrandizement? How now do we build pyramids? There is a new way. It is a way the ancients, the Pharaohs, with no science of banking, could not have imagined. The name of it is credit. In our world, a world of money economy, command of credit is the command of labor and materials. There may be intervening complexities, the obvious may be obscured, yet in every case that is what it comes to at last; and, in fact, people have no other use for credit.

Borrowing and lending are as old as the sense of mine and thine; therefore, so is credit in the simple term. But modern credit as we know it, or think we know it, is a new and amazing power, still evolving, still untamed. Men have been much more anxious to release the power of credit, to employ and exploit it, than to control it or even

to understand it. That would be only human. As formerly
there was no aggrandizement, private or public, without a
Pharaoh-like command of labor and materials, so now
there is none without command of credit.

This holds for aggrandizement in any dimension. The
very magnitude of human life in the present earth is
owing to the power of credit. The whole of our industrial phenomena is founded on it. By means of credit
the machine is created in the first place; by means of
credit the machine is manned and moved and fed with
raw materials. By means of credit the product of machines
is distributed. By means of credit more and more this
product is consumed, as when credit is loaned at home
to the instalment buyer or loaned abroad to the foreign
customer. Thus the power of credit is employed dynam-
ically in the aggrandizement of trade, wherein are many
dangers yet to be explored, such as those of wild inflation
and deflation, followed by sudden crisis. The greed of
individuals and groups, the extravagances of civic ego, the
ambition of nations, ideas creative and destructive both,
great social ends and great fallacies at the same time,
even war—credit for all of these is the fabulous agent.
And then, besides, with any motive, it builds pyramids,
which is the singular point and the one we are after.

That is the one thing credit is supposed not to do. The
restraining principles are interest and amortization. To
amortize a debt is to redeem it, to extinguish it finally,
or, literally, put it to death. Debt we have not mentioned.
Most of the follies we commit with the power of credit
are from forgetting that debt is the other face of credit.
There is no credit but with an exact equivalent of debt.
That is to say, when by means of credit you command
labor and materials, you borrow them and become a
debtor. As a debtor you must pay interest, so much per
annum, on what you have borrowed, and sometime later
return the principal, which puts the debt to death. We
suppose commonly that interest and amortization concern

only the borrower and lender. Who lends money will demand something for the use of it while he himself is doing without it, and surety for its return after a certain time. That is so; but that is not all of it.

From the point of view of the total social organism, interest and amortization have a kind of functional significance. They are the only two checks we have upon the universal passion to abuse the power of credit, or to waste in reckless and uneconomic ways the labor that is by credit commanded.

The borrower is expected to say: "This thing I propose to create with credit will be in turn creative. I mean it will be productive and give increase. Out of the increase I will pay interest for use of the credit; out of the increase I will extinguish the debt. The remainder I will keep for my own as profit."

He may say that of a steel works, a textile factory, a railroad, an electric-power plant, of ten thousand and one things you may not think of; he cannot say it of a pyramid.

Precisely, therefore, the function of interest and amortization, beyond any private concern of either borrower or lender, is to restrain pyramid building. Nevertheless, it will be perceived that the modern world is magnificent with pyramids. Where Pharaoh built one by tyrannical command of labor and materials, credit now builds thousands. You are not to look for them in the exact shape of Pharaoh's. Ours are in shapes of endless variety, many of them apparent, some not so apparent because they present a specious aspect of usefulness, and some invisible. The invisible kind are of all the most devouring.

Taking them by kinds, what are they—our pyramids? The most obvious to perception are those in the category of public works, such as monumental buildings, erections to civic grandeur, ornate boulevards, stadiums, recreation centers, communal baths, and so on. Here, to begin with, the restraining function of interest and amortization is relaxed. It is not said that works in this character will be productive. It is said that they will contribute to the happiness and comfort of people, which is their justification, and it is generally true. And it is said, moreover: "Why should people wait until they can have saved the money for this extension of their happiness and comfort when they may have it immediately on credit? They will tax themselves to pay interest on the debt and to pay the principal of the debt as it comes due."

But so even with pyramids in this very desirable meaning, let the impatience for them become extravagant and reckless, as it will and does, and let too much labor be moved by credit to the making of them all at once, and you may be sure of what will happen. To pay interest on the debt and then to pay the debt itself taxes will rise until people cannot afford to pay them. That is what they will say. But the reason they cannot afford to pay taxes is that they could not afford those very desirable unproductive things to begin with. Either they did not know this in time or they did not care. They may repudiate the debt, yet as you may consider society in the whole that will make no difference whatever, since it remains true that society in the whole is wanting all those other exchangeable human satisfactions, more important than sights and diversions, that might have been produced with the same labor in place of those well-intentioned and premature pyramids.

In another category are things that afterward turn into pyramids. This will happen when those by whom the credit was commanded have used it with bad judgment, or too much of it for a given result, or dishonestly, or to create a thing for which after all there is no demand, so that what they were pursuing was not a reality within reason of probability but a delusion of profit—and pursuing it with other people's labor, other people's money. Yet the thing itself may be magnificent, like the tallest skyscraper in a great city, so marvellous in its architectural and engineering features that people will come from great distances away for the thrill of looking at it. Whether or not in such a case given, the entire motive was profit, free of any will to aggrandizement, it is profit or loss that will determine the economic status of each new piece of wonder. If there is profit, if it can pay interest and put the debt to death out of its earnings, or, that is to say, if it can return to the common reservoir the credit that was borrowed, then it is not a pyramid. It is a thing productive, giving increase. But if there is loss, so that interest and amortization cannot be met out of the increase, out of the earnings, out of the rents, then and exactly in the measure to which this is true, the thing is a pyramid. We say in that case the capital is lost. But what the loss of capital means is that the labor is lost, and again, no matter who specifically takes the loss, society as a whole is wanting all the imaginable other satisfactions that might have been produced in place of this pyramid.

By the same definition, the overbuilding of industry beyond any probable demand for the product represents devoured credit. Here the spirit of aggrandizement acts as if it were a biological law, each separate organization trying to outgrow all the others of its own kind in the industry of one country, and then that industry as a whole in one country trying to outgrow the competitive industry of another country, and this going on with benefit of more and more credit, until at last—what is the problem? The problem is that so much credit, that is to say labor, is trapped, frozen, locked up in the world's industrial machine, that people cannot afford to buy the whole of its product at prices which will enable industry to pay interest on its debt. This is perhaps the most involved form of pyramid that human ingenuity has yet devised.

To see it clearly, you may have to push it to the focus of extreme absurdity. Suppose, for example, that half of all the capital in the world were invested in shoe-making machinery. You have there the capacity to make in one

day many more shoes than there are feet in the world,
and yet the necessity to pay interest on half the capital in
the world and charge it to the price of shoes will make
shoes so dear that nobody can afford to buy them. The
answer is that all the capital invested in excess shoe-
making machinery is lost. Nearly half the capital in the
world! Half less the relatively small amount that may be
properly so invested. Exactly. It is really lost. The labor
it represents is lost. All the wanted things that this labor
might have produced in place of that excess of shoe-making machinery—they are lost, and forever lost. You cannot recover the labor by unbuilding the machinery any
more than Pharaoh could have recovered his wasted
Egyptian labor by unbuilding the pyramid.

Then the invisible pyramids—what are they?

A delirious stock-exchange speculation such as the one
that went crash in 1929 is a pyramid of that character.
Its stones are avarice, mass-delusion and mania; its
tokens are bits of printed paper representing fragments
and fictions of title to things both real and unreal, including title to profits that have not yet been earned and
never will be. All imponderable. An ephemeral, whirling,
upside-down pyramid, doomed in its own velocity. Yet it
devours credit in an uncontrollable manner, more and
more to the very end; credit feeds its velocity.

In two years brokers' loans on the New York Stock
Exchange alone increased five billions of dollars. That
was credit borrowed by brokers on behalf of speculators,
and it was used to inflate the daily Stock Exchange quotations for those bits of printed paper representing fragments and fictions of title to things both real and unreal.
It was credit that might have been used for productive
purposes. The command of labor and materials represented by that amount of credit would have built an
express highway one hundred feet wide from New York
to San Francisco and then one from Chicago to Mexico
City, with something over. Or taking wages at six dollars

a day, it represents more than the six hundred million days of man power wasted by Pharaoh on his Cheops. But the use of it to inflate Stock Exchange prices added not one dollar of real wealth to the country.

You may think that since it was all a delusion on the profit side, the loss also must have been imaginary; that if nothing was added to the wealth of the country, neither was anything taken away. But that is not the way of it. First there was the direct loss of diverting that credit from all the possible uses of production to the unproductive use of speculation. Secondly, a great deal of it was consumed by two or three million speculators, large and small, who, with that rich feeling upon them, borrowed money on their paper profits and spent it. In this refinement of procedure what happens is that imaginary wealth is exchanged for real wealth; and the real wealth is consumed by those who have produced nothing in place of it. Thirdly—and this was the terrific loss—the shock from the headlong fall of this pyramid caused all the sensitive sources and streams and waters of credit to contract in fear. The more they contracted the more fear there was, the more fear the more contraction, effect acting upon cause. The sequel was abominable panic.

This is only the most operatic example of the pyramid invisible. Such a thing must be any artificial or inflated price structure, requiring credit to support it. The Federal Farm Board built two great pyramids in agriculture, one in wheat and one in cotton, and named them stabilization. It was using government credit, borrowed from the people, to support wheat and cotton prices. Nevertheless, wheat and cotton prices were bound to fall, and that credit was lost. There has been a vogue for pyramids by the name of stabilization. Scores of them have been built, private and public, all using credit in a more or less desperate effort to support prices that were bound for natural reasons to fall.

Foreign trade inflated by the credit we loaned to our foreign customers—that was a grand pyramid of a special kind, half visible and half invisible, partly real and partly unreal. The trade was visible; the idea of profit in it was largely a delusion. Almost we forgot that we were buying this trade with our own credit.

Moreover, of total loans out of the American credit reservoir to foreign countries, amounting grossly to fifteen billions of dollars, a great deal of it has been used not to inflate foreign trade but by the foreign borrowers to build pyramids of their own at our expense. This magnificent oddity, here only to be mentioned, will return in its due place.

A certain confusion may now be beginning to rise. Credit, again, regarded simply as a command of labor and materials. In that definition the mind makes no difficulty about relating it to ponderable things, such as pyramids in the form of public works or excess industrial capacity, for these are only certain physical objects in place of others that might have been wrought with the instrumentality of that same credit; it may, however, find some difficulty in relating it to imponderable things also called pyramids, such as a Wall Street ecstasy. For how does credit originate? Whose is it to begin with? How is command of it acquired? How does it get from where it originates to where it is found producing its prodigious effects?

All of this may be seen, and will be easier to do than you would think. To see credit rising at its source, to see whose it is to begin with, to see how it moves from the spring to the stream and then anywhere, even to the maelstrom, and to see at the same time Sumner's Forgotten Man, you have only to go to the nearest bank and sit there for half an hour in an attitude of attention. Any bank will do. The first one you come to.

Observe first the physical arrangements. There will be along the counter a series of little windows, each with a legend over it. Above one window it will be "Savings." Over the next two or three it will be "Teller." Then one,

"Discounts and Collections." And at one side, where the counter ends, you will see behind a railing several desks with little metal plates on them, one saying "President," another "Vice President," and another "Cashier," unless it is a very small bank, in which case the cashier will be behind one of the windows.

Then observe the people and what they come to do. Some go straight to the window marked "Savings." These all bring money to leave with the bank at interest. One is a man in overalls. That is wage money to be saved. Another is a farmer's wife, and that may be milk or butter money. Next the poultry man with some profit to be put aside. Then two or three housewives, evidently, such as regularly include in their budgets a sum to be saved. After these a foreman from the railroad and a garage mechanic, and so on. Each one puts money between the leaves of a little book and pushes it through the window; the man there counts it, writes the amount in the little book and pushes the book back to the depositor. That goes on all day. At the day's end all the money received at this window is counted, bundled and tossed into the safe, and then written down in the big book of the bank as "Time Deposits."

Those who go to the windows marked "Teller" are somewhat different. They represent local trade, commerce and industry. Their accounts are current, called checking accounts or credit balances. They bring both cash and checks to deposit; and besides making deposits they may tender their own checks to be cashed, often at the same time. For example, the man who owns the sash and blind factory brings nothing but checks to deposit; everybody owing him money has paid him by check. But he hires ten men and this is pay day. Therefore, needing cash to pay wages, he writes his own check for the amount of his pay roll and receives that sum in cash. But this money he takes away presently comes back to the bank through other hands. The employees of the sash and blind factory spend it with the grocer and butcher and department-store keeper who immediately bring it to the bank and deposit it at the "Teller" windows where it came from. What the employees of the sash and blind factory do not spend they themselves bring back to the bank and leave at the window marked "Savings." Such is the phenomenon called the circulation of money. The same dollar may go out of the bank and return again two or three times in one week. The speed with which a dollar performs its work and returns to the bank is called the velocity of money.

At the end of the day the men at the "Teller" windows count up in one column what they have received and in another what they have paid out, and the difference is written down in the bank's books as an increase or decrease of "Demand Deposits." The rule is that more will have been received than was paid out, so there is normally each day an increase of deposits. It is normal that all these people representing local business should bring to the "Teller" windows more than they take away, because their activities are severally productive, giving always some increase, more or less according to the state of the times.

Well, then, this daily increase of "Demand Deposits" from the "Teller" windows is tossed into the safe, along with those "Time Deposits" from the window marked "Savings." Thus the bank accumulates deposits—that is to say, money. What does it do with the money? A bank pays interest; therefore, a bank must earn interest. It must earn more interest than it pays out, else it cannot make a profit for itself. So the bank must lend its deposits. To receive money on which it pays interest and to lend money on which it receives interest—that is a bank's whole business.

Now, what proportion of its total deposits do you suppose a bank lends? How much would you think it was safe to lend? The half? Three quarters? All? The fact is —and even those who know it well and take it for granted

are astonished in those moments when they stop to reflect
on it—the fabulous fact is that a bank may lend ten times
its deposits. That is to say, for each actual dollar of other
people's money it has received and locked up in its safe,
it may lend or sell ten dollars of credit money.

Not every bank does lend ten to one—ten dollars of
credit to one of cash in the vault; but if you take the
banking system entire it has the potential power to erect
credit in that ratio to cash. Ten to one was the formula
adopted by the United States Treasury and other Federal
Government agencies in their campaign against hoarding. In official messages broadcast over the country people
were exhorted to stop hoarding and bring their money
back to the banks on the ground that each dollar of actual
money in hiding represented a loss of ten in the credit
resources of the country, and that each dollar of money
brought back to the banks represented an increase of ten
dollars in credit for the common benefit of trade, commerce and industry.

The beginning of all modern credit phenomena is in
this act of multiplication, performed by the banker. How
can a bank lend credit to the amount of ten times its cash
deposits?

Perhaps the easiest way to explain it will be to tell
the story of the old goldsmiths who received gold for safe
keeping and issued receipts for it. These receipts, representing the gold, began to pass from hand to hand as
money. Seeing this, and that people seldom touched the
gold itself or wanted it back, so long as they thought it
was safe, the goldsmiths began to issue paper redeemable
in gold, without having the gold in hand to redeem it
with. A very audacious idea. And yet it was sound, or at
least it worked, and if a goldsmith was honest he was
solvent because in exchange for that paper, which he
promised to redeem in gold on demand, he took things of
value, called collateral, in pledge, so that against his outstanding paper he had good assets in hand, and if people

did come with his paper, wanting the gold on it, he had only to sell those assets, buy the gold, then redeem the paper according to his promise—always provided the assets were liquid and easily sold and that too many people never came at once, all demanding gold on the instant. Fewer and fewer people ever did want the actual gold. So long as they believed in the goldsmith they preferred to use his paper for all purposes of exchange—paper which no longer represented the actual gold and yet was as good as gold and was counted as gold because whenever anybody did want the gold it was forthcoming. From this evolved modern banking. That circulating paper itself became legal money against which the banks were obliged by law and custom to keep a certain amount of gold in hand, called the gold reserve. The next step was to discover that upon this structure of legal paper money with a gold reserve behind it you could impose another strata of paper—a new free kind, redeemable either in gold or legal paper money. That new free kind of paper was the bank check we all know; and the use of bank checks in place of actual money has increased by habit and necessity until now we transact more than nine tenths of all our business by check, no actual money passing at all, or almost none. In the year 1929, for example, the total amount of actual money of all kinds in the country was nine billions; but the total exchange of bank checks was 713 billions, or nearly eighty times all the actual money in existence.

What a bank now lends is credit in the form of a blank check book. You use the credit by writing checks against it. You may write a check for cash and draw out actual money in the form of gold or legal paper money, but if you do and spend the money it will go straight back to the bank. When you borrow at the bank, what happens? The banker does not hand you the money. He writes down in the bank's own book a certain credit to your account and gives you a book of blank checks. Then you go out and begin to write checks against that credit. The people to whom you give the checks deposit them in the bank. As they deposit your checks the sums are charged to your account, deducted from your credit on the books. No actual money is involved.

If these last few passages have been difficult, take the fact lightly and without blame. Of all the discoveries and inventions by which we live and die this totally improbable helix of credit is the most cunning, the most liable, the least comprehended and, next to high explosives, the most dangerous. All that bankers themselves really know about it is how it works from day to day. Beyond that it is a gift from Pandora.

But you are still sitting in the local bank. Take it, if necessary, as an arbitrary fact that for each dollar of actual money that passes inward through those windows and stops in the safe the bank will have six, eight, maybe ten dollars of credit to lend. To whom does it lend this credit? And how?

There is a window yet to be observed, the one marked "Discounts and Collections." The transactions at this window take more time. Papers are signed and exchanged. These people are borrowers; they are attending to their loans, paying them off, or paying something on account, or arranging to have their promissory notes extended. One is the local contractor who has had to have credit on his note to pay for materials and labor while building a house; the house is finished, he has been paid by the owner, and now he returns the credit by paying off his note—with a check. Another is the local automobile dealer who has just received from Detroit a carload of automobiles with draft attached, and the draft reads, "Pay at once." To pay the draft he must borrow credit at the bank; as he sells the automobiles one by one in the community he will return the credit—by check. Another is the radio dealer who sells radios on the instalment plan. He is borrowing credit against which he will write a

check to pay the radio manufacturer for ten sets; as security for the loan he gives his own promissory note, together
with the ten purchase contracts of the ten local people to
whom he has sold the radio sets. As they pay him he will
pay the bank—by check. Another is a farmer who has
sold his crop and now is paying back—by check—the
credit he borrowed six months ago to buy fertilizer and
some new farm machinery.

Lending of this character, to local people, the bank
knowing all of them personally, is not only the safest kind
of lending for the bank; it is the ideal use of credit. Unfortunately, the local demand for credit is not enough to
absorb the bank's whole lending power. From the savings
of the community, always accumulating in the safe as cash
deposits, the bank acquires a surplus lending power.
Having satisfied its own customers with credit at the
window marked "Discounts and Collections", what will
the bank do with the surplus credit? Well, now you will
see how credit, so rising at the obscure local source, over-
flows the source and begins to seek outlets to the lakes and
gulfs and seas beyond—how its adventures begin.

The first thing the bank thinks to do with a part of its
surplus credit is to lend it to a big New York City bank.
What will the New York bank do with it? The New
York bank may lend it to a merchant in domestic trade
or to one in the foreign trade; it may lend it to a broker
on the Stock Exchange who lends it to a speculator; it
may lend it in Europe to the Bank of England or it may
lend it to a German bank where the interest rate is very
high. Fancy local American credit, originating as you
have seen, finding its way from this naïve source to a
Berlin bank! Well, several hundreds of millions of just
that kind of American credit did find its way to the banks
of Germany and got trapped there in 1931. The German
banks said they could not pay it back. That was what
the moratorium was all about. Germany said if we insisted on having our credit back, her banks would simply

shut up; she advised us to "freeze" it and leave it there on deposit in the German banks, in the hope that they might be able later to pay, and since there was nothing else to do we did that.

What else will the local bank do with its surplus credit? It will buy a United States government bond; it is simply lending this local credit to the Federal Government.

What will the Federal Government do with it? The Federal Government may give it to the Federal Farm Board to support those wheat and cotton pyramids; the Federal Government may give it to the Reconstruction Finance Corporation, which will lend it to the railroads; the Federal Government may give it to the Veterans' Bureau, which will lend it to war veterans, or the Federal Government may spend it either to finish the memorial bridge across the Potomac River at Washington or for paper and lead pencils to be distributed on the desks of the Senate and House.

But the local bank has still a surplus of credit to lend. So far, by all the rules, it has been very conservative. The credit it has loaned to the big New York City bank is returnable on call. No worry about that. To get back the credit it has loaned to the United States Government it has only to sell the bond, and there is always an instant market for government bonds. So now the bank thinks it may take some risk, for the sake of obtaining a higher rate of interest.

You may notice a man talking very earnestly to the president at the desk behind the railing, and from something you read in his gestures you may take him to be a salesman. That is what he is—a bond salesman from Wall Street, and his merchandise this time is foreign bonds. He has some South American government bonds that pay seven per cent. and some German municipal bonds that pay eight per cent., and these are very attractive rates of interest, seeing that the bank pays its depositors only three and one half.

"You may think," the salesman is saying to the president, "that such rates of interest as seven and eight per cent. imply some risk in these bonds. Really there is no risk. The bonds are absolutely good. Foreign borrowers have to pay high rates of interest in this country, not because they are anything but good and solvent borrowers, but because our people are strange to foreign investments. That being temporarily so, this is a rare opportunity for a little bank like yours to make some very profitable investments."

So persuaded, the local bank with the remainder of its surplus credit buys foreign bonds. When it buys the bond of a South American Government, it is lending credit to that government, knowing no more about it than the salesman says. What will the South American Government do with that credit? Anything it likes, because it is a sovereign government; it may use it to build a gilded dome. Many new gilt domes have been built in foreign countries with just this kind of local American credit.

In buying the German bonds the bank is lending credit to the Free City of Bremen, perhaps, or to Cologne. What does the Free City of Bremen do with it? She may use it to widen the fairway of her harbor and build some new piers. The same credit might have been used to make ship channels and piers in the Hackensack Meadows of New Jersey. And what does Cologne do with it? She may use it to build a stadium or a great bathing pavilion for the happiness and comfort of her people. How strange! The local American community out of which this credit rises to perform such works in Germany has neither stadium nor swimming pool of its own. Or Cologne may use it to help build the largest new bridge in Europe across the Rhine, a bridge she really does not need, except to provide employment for her people. The same credit might be used to build a bridge across the Golden Gate at San Francisco.

One last observation before you leave the bank. How

remote these people are from what is doing with the credit that rises from the dollars they leave at the windows! How little they know about it! Fancy telling that woman at the "Savings" window, who gets her money up in small bills from the deeps of an old satchel, that her dollars, multiplied ten times by the bank, will go to build ornaments for a grand boulevard in a little Latin-American country she never heard of, or to build workmen's houses in a German city better than the house she lives in. Fancy telling the man in overalls who comes next that his money, multiplied ten times by the bank, will go to a speculator on the New York Stock Exchange, or to mend a cathedral in Bavaria, or to a foreign bank that may lose it unless the matter of reparations is somehow settled in Europe, or that it may be loaned to Germany in order that Germany may pay reparations to the Allies in order that they may be willing to pay something on account of what they owe to the United States Treasury.

Remember as you leave the bank that it was one of 25,000, big and little, all performing the same act of multiplication, all in the same general ways lending the product of multiplication, which is credit. You have seen only one spring in the woods. Think of 25,000 such springs in the land, all continually overflowing with credit, and how this surplus local credit, seeking interest, by a law as unerring as the force of gravity finds its way to the streams that lead away to the lakes, gulfs and seas beyond. If you will keep this picture in suspense, you will better understand what else happens, if and when it does—and it is bound to happen from a reckless or deluded use of the power of credit.

There is a change in the economic heavens. Some stars fall out. On the ground some pyramids collapse. For two or three weeks what the Wall Street reporters call a debacle on the Stock Exchange holds first-page news position. Then one day a New York City bank with 400,000 depositors must paste a piece of paper in its plate-glass window, saying: "Closed by order of the State Bank Examiner." Of the surplus credit rising from the cash deposits of its forgotten 400,000 that bank has loaned too much on things such as afterward turn out to be pyramids—for example, skyscrapers.

Do you remember the old lady with the satchel at the window marked "Savings" in the small local bank? She has a friend in New York City who was one of the 400,000. She gets a letter from this friend, saying a bank these days is no place for one's money. It will be safer, even though without interest, in many places a woman can think of. It may be the bottom of the flour can. So this old lady appears again at the window marked "Savings." She wants all her money out. Then the man in overalls comes; he has heard something to the same effect and he wants all of his money out. These two would not matter to the great American banking system as a whole. But remember, this is one of 25,000 banks, in each one of which a few depositors are asking for their money back, all at one time. This, then, is the beginning of that contraction in all the springs and streams and waters of credit that was spoken of before.

What now takes place is the reverse of multiplication. It is deflation. The banker cannot control it. If he has multiplied credit in the ratio of ten for one, so, as his depositors take away their money, he must reduce credit in the same ratio. That is to say, for each dollar of cash that is taken out of his hands, he must call back from somewhere ten dollars of credit. Thus the vast and sensitive mechanism of credit, running at high speed, is put suddenly in reverse motion, with a frightful clashing of gears.

Return to the case of the little local bank, where you were sitting. As its depositors continue to withdraw cash, it must call in credit. First it sends word by telephone or telegraph to the big New York City bank, saying: "Please return our credit. We need it."

But since the New York bank, remember, has loaned that credit out, it must in turn call it back from some one else. If it has loaned it on the Stock Exchange to brokers, who have loaned it to speculators, these must give it back. But suppose the New York City banks that supply the Stock Exchange with credit are all calling at the same time for it to be returned, because thousands of local banks all over the country, where the credit came from, are calling upon them to return it.

In that case the Stock Exchange brokers are sunk. They cannot replace the credit they are called upon to give up, because the sources of credit are now contracting. This being the fact, the brokers say to their customers, namely, the speculators: "We are sorry and this is awful, but there is no more credit. The banks are calling our loans. We cannot carry your securities any longer on credit. If you cannot pay for them in cash in the next fifteen minutes, we shall have to sell them for what they will bring, to save ourselves."

From this cause there is a new day of panic on the Stock Exchange, a further debacle, with hideous wide headlines in the papers. Panic is advertised. The whirling Stock Exchange pyramid is falling, for want of credit to sustain it. This is an effect that becomes in turn a cause. Because of the headlong decline in prices on the Stock Exchange, in which the loss of imaginary wealth is measured, and for other reasons not exactly given, more banks fail. Each day the lines of anxious depositors grow longer. Thus the waters of credit continue to contract, and the rate is accelerated.

But suppose the New York bank has loaned the credit to a bank in Berlin and cannot get it back at all. What will it do in that case? For it is obliged either to return the credit to the small local bank that is demanding it back or confess itself insolvent. Well, in that case the New York bank must sell some securities out of its own reserve investments. But if all the New York banks are

doing the same thing at the same time, as more or less they
will be, the effect on the Stock Exchange is even worse.
The banks will be selling bonds where speculators would
be selling only stocks, and the effect upon the mind of
the country from a fall in bonds is much more disturbing.

Now what you are looking at is liquidation. Credit is
contracting because these thousands of forgotten bank depositors are calling for their money; and because credit
is contracting everybody is calling at once for the return
of it to its source, and there is no way for the person who
last borrowed to return it but to sell something.

Suppose, however, that the local bank gets its credit
back from the New York bank. It is not enough. Its depositors continue to take their money out; more credit
must be called in—always, remember, ten for one. Some-
body, somewhere, must give up ten dollars of credit for
each dollar of actual money the depositors withdraw. The
local bank next thinks of selling its South American
bonds. That is another way of calling credit back. Some-
body will have to buy the bonds, of course, but that simply
means that whoever buys them from the bank will be
taking the bank's place as creditor of the South American
Government that issued the bonds. The bank need not
worry about who that buyer is; the transaction will take
place in the open bond market, where the law of *caveat
emptor* holds. Buyer, beware.

But when the local bank goes to sell its South American
bonds it finds them quoted at thirty—the same bonds it
paid ninety for. The South American Government is in
financial trouble, and all the buyers standing in the bond
market know it; that is why they will offer only thirty
for the bonds. If the bank sells them at thirty it will have
lost forever two thirds of the credit it loaned to the
South American Government. Besides, if that is all it can
get for the bonds, it will not greatly help to sell them. So
it puts these bonds aside and looks at its German bonds.

But German bonds also have collapsed. Their condition may be as bad, or worse, because Germany is in trouble. What else can the bank sell? It can sell its United States government bonds; yet even in these there is a considerable loss. They have declined in price under the selling of hundreds, thousands, of other banks all in the same dilemma, all tempted to sell their United States government bonds instead of worse bonds on which they cannot afford to take the loss.

Having got back the credit it loaned to the United States Government, by selling its United States government bonds, the local bank goes on for a while, paying off its depositors, exhorting them to desist, telling them everything will be all right, hoping for the best. Then one day the Bank Examiner from the Comptroller's office at Washington comes unexpectedly to look at the books and decide if the bank is solvent. Having looked at the books he says: "See here! You have sold all of your best assets. Now to make your books balance with bad assets you still value them at what you paid for them. These foreign bonds, for example—still valued on your books at ninety and ninety-five when you know very well they are worth in the market to-day only thirty or thirty-five. You are not a solvent bank. You will have to close."

Then the fatal piece of white paper is pasted on the plate glass, and all the depositors then at the windows asking for their money are put out.

That—almost exactly that—happened to 3,635 banks of all kinds in the two years 1930 and 1931. The deposits of these 3,635 ruined banks were more than 2½ billions of dollars.

It is easily forgotten that the depositor who stands outside to read the Bank Examiner's verdict through the glass was the original lender.

Consider what it is a depositor does. It is clear enough that when he makes a deposit he is lending money to the bank. But what does the money represent? If it is earned

money the depositor brings, it represents something of
equal value produced by his own exertions, something he
would sooner save than consume. It may be a cord of
wood. Suppose it.

There are only a few things to do with a surplus cord of
wood. If you store it for your own future use it represents
earned leisure. If you exchange it with a neighbor for
something else you want that is conversion by crude
barter. In neither case is there any increase. It is all the
time one cord of wood. You may sell it for money. If you
hoard the money you have the equivalent of one cord of
wood and yet no increase. But suppose you take the money
to the bank and leave it there at interest. In that case you
have loaned the bank your surplus labor to the value of a
cord of wood, and there is the beginning of increase. Another industrious man, who is without tools, borrows
money from the bank to buy an ax, a maul and some
wedges. These tools represent your cord of wood. With
these tools that man chops three cords of wood. One he
wants for himself and two he sells. With the proceeds of
one he returns to the bank the money he borrowed to buy
the tools. He has still in his hand the proceeds of the
third cord, which is profit or increase. Let him resolve,
instead of spending the increase, to save it. He puts
it in the bank. Now the bank has two cords of wood
where there was but one before—not the cordwood itself,
not the labor itself, but the money agent of labor; besides
which are the tools still in the man's hand. All this from
one surplus cord of wood to begin with.

Thus we accumulate wealth, and there is no limit to
it, provided the labor is not lost.

Now suppose a third man comes and borrows all of
that money to build a toy in the meaning of a pyramid
that has no economic value, or to make an unlucky speculation, or to buy something he is impatient to enjoy before
he has produced anything of equivalent value and then
afterward fails to produce the equivalent, so that it turns

out that he is unable to pay interest or return the principal. We say in that case the money is lost. Really it is not. It still exists. But what the money represented is lost, and that was the amount of labor necessary to produce two cords of wood.

There is neither value nor power in money itself, only in what it represents. Every dollar of actual money should betoken that a dollar's worth of wealth has been somewhere in some form produced; every dollar of credit multiplied upon that money by the banker should signify that somewhere in some form a dollar's worth of wealth is in process of creation.

Anything that happens to money to debase it, to degrade its relation to the total sum of wealth, so as to impair its buying power, is something that happens to people who have loaned their labor to the banks.

Why do we confine the function of money issue to the government, and have very rigid laws concerning the exercise of that function by the government, and make counterfeiting a crime? All that is with the idea of keeping the value of money constant, for if money is permitted to increase faster than the wealth of things which we price in money, then the value of labor saved in the form of money will deteriorate like a cord of wood in the weather. When for any reason a government is moved to embrace legal counterfeiting, when it begins to issue spurious money—money that has no definite relation to any form of wealth in being or in process—the sequel is well known. There is progressive inflation, which, once it begins, there is no stopping or controlling, short of the final disaster. At the end, the savings of a lifetime, reconverted into money, may not be enough to buy a hat.

This we have learned about money itself, dimly. We have yet to learn it about credit, even dimly.

To any suggestion that the government shall set its printing presses free and flood the country with fiat money, all our economic intelligence reacts with no. Only those will say yes who are mentally or politically unsound. And if a government is obliged by vote of the unsound to do it, then everybody, including the unsound, will begin to hoard gold because gold is the one kind of money no government can make or dilute. Or if it were proposed that every bank should have the privilege to issue money as it might think fit, entirely in its own discretion, we should all know better. Even banks would say no to that. It is not only that people cannot trust private bankers with that privilege; private bankers would be unwilling to trust one another with it.

Yet on this jealously guarded base of money itself, banks are free to inflate and multiply credit, each in its own discretion, notwithstanding the fact that the inflation of money and the inflation of credit are similar evils, producing similar miseries. Inflation of credit—ecstasy, delusion, fantastic enrichment. Deflation of credit—depression, crisis, remorse. One state succeeds the other and there is no escape, for one is cause and one is effect.

ON SAVING EUROPE

(THE MORATORIUM)

"A little debt makes a debtor, but a great one an enemy."
—GNOMOLOGIA

Take a text from the news as it was printed in the *New York Times* on Monday, June 23, 1931: "Led by New York, tremendous buying enthusiasm swept over the security and commodity markets of the world yesterday in response to week-end developments reflecting the favorable reception of President Hoover's proposal for a one-year moratorium on war debts and reparations. The world-wide advance in prices added billions of dollars to open market values, with stocks, bonds, grain, cotton, sugar, silver and lead in heavy demand. Pronounced strength developed in the German bond list, the gains ranging from 2 to 13½ points. . . . United States government bonds failed to participate in the move, all of them closing behind minus signs."

The last line fell obscurely at the end of a paragraph. And that was all the notice any one bestowed upon the most significant fact of a delirious day, namely, the fact that everything in the world went up with the single exception of United States government bonds. And why was that? United States government bonds were telling why, and telling it loudly to such as would listen. They were telling it in the language of quotations, and this is what they were saying:

"Again this business of saving Europe with American credit! Do you ever count up what it has cost you already?

It is becoming more and more costly; and, besides, you may not be saving Europe at all. You may be only inflating her. Better may turn out to be worse."

As it did. The world-wide rise in everything but United States government bonds was fictitious, a momentary delusion. Worse was to come.

Specifically, the Hoover debt holiday plan was to save Germany from financial collapse and so avert a disaster that had been bound to react in a ghastly manner upon the whole structure of international finance. The first cost to us was reckoned at $250,000,000. That was the sum we should have to forego on account of war debts owing by Great Britain, France, Belgium, Italy and others to the American Treasury. We could not propose simply that Germany should stop paying reparations for a year to her European creditors. That would have cost Great Britain, France, Belgium, Italy and others too much. They could not afford it. If they had to forego reparations from Germany and still pay interest to the United States Treasury on their American war debts they would be hurt in their pockets. So what we proposed was that if Germany's European creditors would give her one year of grace on reparations, the United States would give them one year of grace on their war debt payments to the American Treasury.

Even so there were difficulties, because it would still cost Europe herself something to save Germany. The situation was that France, Great Britain, Belgium and others had been collecting as reparations from Germany a little more than $400,000,000 a year and paying the United States on account of their war debts to the American Treasury a little less than $250,000,000 a year. Thus a general international war debt holiday to save Germany would cost them the difference, or about $150,000,000. Great Britain had been collecting from her war debtors only $50,000,000 more than she had been paying to the United States on account of her own American war debt;

and she was willing. But France had been collecting from Germany $100,000,000 more than she had been paying to the United States Treasury on account of her war debt, and she was unwilling. After long and painful negotiations it was agreed, for the sake of the debt holiday plan and to save Germany, that France should receive special treatment. An irreducible portion of her reparations money would be paid by Germany to the International Bank at Basle and then reloaned by France to Germany under a new arrangement. Everybody else took Germany's word for it.

Thus the plan took effect. It cost us $250,000,000. Well, a little more. While Germany's European creditors were debating the plan and higgling over what it was going to cost them, the Federal Reserve Bank in New York made a direct loan to the German Reichsbank to keep it open. Say, then, it had cost us altogether $300,-000,000. Was it not cheap?

We really thought we had done a grand thing; we read every morning in the newspapers that it was a grand thing. The diplomats and chancelleries of Europe were saying so, on typewritten slips, or in interviews, and the American correspondents were quoting them to us by cable. But the typewritten words of diplomats and chancelleries are purposefully suave. What people were really thinking and saying, even the diplomats, was very different. They were saying, among other things: "This is the beginning of the end of our hateful war debts to the U(ncle) S(hylock) Treasury."

Conservative British newspapers did play up to the official Downing Street tune, the more willingly because it happened to be the British season for hating France; all the popular papers were sarcastic.

French opinion was caustic. These Americans, always saying they wouldn't and didn't, now again blundering their hands into the affairs of Europe, not understanding them at all. Interfering without knowing what it was they

interfered with. Using their power of credit to dictate
terms between France and Germany. Why shouldn't they
lend their credit as credit merely, in a financial way, and
otherwise mind their own business? Besides, they were in
bad manners, as usual, to propose that France should
forego German reparations for a year without having first
consulted France about it.

Comment in Germany was brutal and a little exultant.
The Americans were obliged to save Germany from bankruptcy in order to protect the two and one half billions or
more they had already loaned to her. It was to save themselves they were saving her and saving Europe.

However, we still thought very well of it ourselves. And
in any case, looking at it unromantically, the solvency of
Europe was a bargain at $300,000,000, if really we had
saved it. But in a little while it appeared very clearly that
we hadn't. Within two weeks the whole of that $300,-
000,000 credit had been swallowed up and Europe was
saying to us:

"Now see what has happened! The Hoover plan was
all right; the intention was good. Only it was inade-
quate in the first place, and then, unfortunately, the dila-
tory and public discussion of it by the nations concerned
has advertised Germany's condition to the whole world.
Now all of Germany's private creditors are in a panic.
American banks are calling their deposits out of German
banks. The Germans themselves are in flight from the
mark. What are you going to do about it? If after this
you let Germany go down, it had been better to have done
nothing at all. And if you let Germany go down, all of
Europe may crash."

So there had to be a second Hoover plan to save
Europe. The second plan was that American banks should
stop calling their deposits and short-term credits out of
Germany and relend her the money for a certain period,
say, six months. That meant probably $600,000,000 more
American credit. The cost of saving Germany was sud-

denly multiplied by three. Nevertheless, it had to be done and it was done under the direction of an American banker who was called to Europe for that purpose.

Yet who could say what it was worth to save Germany, first for her own sake and then for the sake of Europe? It was no longer a bargain; still, thinking of the enormous investment of American money in Germany, now all in jeopardy, it might be worth even a billion of dollars—that is to say again, provided we had really saved the situation. But had we? No.

In a few days more it was clear that what all this American credit had bought was only a postponement of evil. The German crisis had still to be met in some radical manner, or else what would happen at the end of the Hoover holiday, or, even before that, when the money perforce reloaned by American banks in Germany for six months was due again? The only radical solution Germany can think of, naturally, is to get rid of reparations; then to borrow more American credit. And the only radical solution the rest of Europe can think of is to get their American war debts cancelled.

But there had been hardly time to begin thinking of radical solutions before another crisis developed. There was an international run on the Bank of England for gold. Her gold began to give out. What could the Old Lady of Threadneedle Street do? What could save the credit of the Bank of England? Only American credit could do that. So the Bank of England came to New York and got a big loan from the Federal Reserve Bank.

American credit had twice saved Germany, once for herself and once for the sake of Europe, and now it had saved the Bank of England—all in less than three months. And the cost had been roughly a billion and a quarter.

Who still could say it had not been worth it?

But again the sigh of relief was interrupted. After all that, another crisis. Germany was not saved; she had been only floated on a raft of American credit. Europe as a whole was not saved because Germany wasn't. And for these reasons the Bank of England discovered immediately that the loan she had got from the Federal Reserve Bank in New York was not enough. That is to say, the Bank of England itself was not saved. She had underestimated the amount of saving required. What to do?

Everybody thought of the same thing at once, as if it were new—the same magic, the same miraculous fluid. More American credit.

But now certain new difficulties. One is that the Bank of England cannot borrow enough. Besides, going to New York again so soon with more I. O. U.'s in her hand will hurt her credit. The American bankers may lift their eyebrows. The next idea is that the British Government itself shall borrow American credit to save the Bank of England. The only weakness of this idea is that the Labor Government of Great Britain as it stands is not in good credit. It is a socialist government and year after year it has been closing the national account book in red ink. It spends so much money upon schemes of social benefit, particularly in the form of a public wage to the unemployed, that it cannot balance its budget. How will it look for the British Government to go asking for American credit when it is already spending more than its income and cannot balance its budget?

American bankers, indeed, had been sounded out to see if they would mind. They had not lifted their eyebrows, but they had said: "Really, before expecting us to float a British loan you ought to do something about your books. They are too much talked about. Can't you economize, spend somewhat less on these meritorious social schemes and balance your budget? If you did that the talk about the red ink in your national account book would stop and then it would be easy enough to float a British loan in America, or to give the British Treasury any amount of bank credit."

Whereupon the British decided to change their government, adopt a program of social economy and balance their budget. This had long been indicated as a necessary thing to do. It was the insolvency of the socialist Labor Government, among other things, that was hurting the credit of the pound sterling. Nevertheless, the disagreeable task of reducing public expenditures was postponed until the Bank of England had exhausted its power to borrow American credit on its I. O. U.'s. Then it became imperative for the British Treasury to put itself in good standing as a borrower.

When the news came from London that the British had changed their government and now were going to balance their budget, Wall Street bankers were already discussing a loan to Great Britain. "They reiterated their preparedness," said the *New York Times,* August 26, "to provide a substantial loan if the new government requires it." Further: "The amount, bankers said, should be as large as can be readily supplied by the banks of the country and the credit should run at least a year. A number of bankers believe Great Britain would benefit from a long-term loan and a few of them believe British credit is still strong enough to make a public offering possible even in the present depressed bond market."

The next day the news in Wall Street was that negotiations had been formally opened and on the third day it was announced that American bankers had loaned the British Treasury $200,000,000 for a year.

But what was the popular reaction in England? The Americans had used their power of credit to interfere in the politics of Great Britain, even to the point of demanding the overthrow of the Labor Government. That was the reaction. The *Daily Herald,* organ of the Labor Party that had been ruling England, said: "Among the reasons Mr. MacDonald advances for imposing new privations on the most unfortunate section of the nation is the 'pressure of public opinion abroad.' Whose opinion? Not that of the democracies of Europe or America, oppressed by unemployment and distress for similar reasons, but that of foreign bankers, who laid down to the British Government terms, including changes in the unemployment benefit scheme, upon which and alone upon which they were prepared to render financial aid to the Bank of England." It said the Federal Reserve Bank of New York had put a pistol to England's head.

Which was to say, the Americans had no right to name the terms on which they would lend their money to save the Bank of England or to save the credit of the British Treasury. They ought to lend their money and mind their own business.

How do people arrive at this ground of unreason—the English people, who before us were the world's principal creditors with a creditor mentality?

It is not simply that political passions have distorted the facts. That is true. But the facts belong to finance and finance is lost in its own world. It knows neither the way to go on nor how to go back. Having raised international debt to a new order of magnitude, now it faces international insolvency of the same grand order, and it is appalled. It cannot manage the facts. The only solution it can think of is more European debt, more American credit. By itself it cannot create any more debt. If the resources of private credit are not quite exhausted, the credulity of the creditor is about to be. But there may be still some resource left in the public credit of Europe. Finance at this point adopts the mentality of the crowd in the street. Let government do it. Let all the European governments increase their debts who can, to save themselves and one another. This is literal.

By agency of international finance Germany, in six or seven years, borrowed nearly four billions of dollars, two thirds of it from American lenders. It was much more than Germany could afford to borrow—that is, if she cared anything at all about her own solvency. Having procured this money to be loaned to Germany, having exhausted every kind of German security that could be made to look like a bond, international finance came to the sequel and said: "Germany must have more credit, for else her whole financial structure will collapse, and if that happens international finance cannot answer for the consequences. They will be terrible. But Germany has no more security to offer. Therefore international finance cannot float another German loan. But if Germany's creditors will collectively guarantee a German bond issue, international finance can float that."

Try going on from there. Suppose Germany's European creditors, namely, Great Britain, France, Italy, Belgium and others should guarantee a German bond issued for more American credit. When that credit was exhausted, what would happen? Perhaps then, in order to go on lending American credit to Europe, we should have to guarantee our own loans. And what better security could you ask? An American loan to Europe guaranteed by Americans!

Well, and what is so very strange about that idea? All the American war loans and all the American post-armistice loans to Europe were guaranteed by the United States Government. It borrowed the money on Liberty Bonds and guaranteed them. If Europe does not pay this debt the American Government will. It cannot be wiped out or cancelled or reduced. It can only be transferred from the European taxpayer to the American taxpayer.

If the American lender is not a menace to the financial sanity of the Old World, the least definition of him would be to say he is to Europe a fabulous enigma.

Critical European economists say we are the worst lenders in the world, because we lend impulsively, in a reckless, emotional manner, not systematically. That is true. It is true that as lenders, simply so regarded, we are incomprehensible to ourselves and to others. Beyond all considerations of an economic or financial character there is pressing upon us continually that strange sense of obligation to save Europe.

It seized us deeply during the war. It carried us into the war. We were going to save Europe from Germany, the German people from the Hohenzollerns, little nations from big ones, all the people of Europe from the curse of war forever. There were other motives, to be sure. We had money on the side of the Allies, though by such measures as we now use it was very little. Our sympathies went to the Allies. We hated the way Germans made war. Some of us may have been a little afraid of a German Europe. Allied propaganda to get us in had its great effect. Yet for all of this we should never have gone in without the emotional thought images that made a crusade of it.

A war to end war. Where? In Europe. A war to make the world safe for democracy. Where was democracy supposed to be in danger? In Europe. A war to liberate oppressed nationalities. Where? In Europe. Not a war against the Germans—we said we had no quarrel with the German people—but a war to deliver them from the tyranny of their own bad war lords. And from no realistic point of view was any of this our business.

The allied nations were not interested in our thought images, or, if at all, in one only because it worried them, and that was the one about saving the weak from the strong, otherwise, the right of self-determination for little people. The Allies did not care what our reasons were. We could be as romantic as we liked, only so we came in on their side, for unless we did the war was lost. They were not themselves fighting to make the world safe for democracy, nor to end war forever, nor to deliver the German people, nor to put destiny into the hands of little people; they were fighting to beat Germany, and with American assistance they did beat her. None of the things we thought we were fighting for came out. What survived was a continuing sense of obligation to save Europe.

Our own exertions in a war we had been much better off to stay out of cost us twenty-five billions of dollars. Then, in addition to that, we loaned out of the United States Treasury more than ten billions to our own associates. Lending to Europe out of the United States Treasury ended with the post-armistice loans. Then private lending began—lending by American banks and American investors. Counting our own direct war expenditures, the war loans, the post-armistice loans, and then the private lending since, Europe has cost us more than forty billions of dollars in less than fifteen years. That sum would have represented one fifth of our total national wealth in the year 1914.

Cast out the cost of our own war exertions. Pass the war loans by the United States Treasury to the Allies out of the proceeds of Liberty Bonds. Say that under the circumstances we were morally obliged to make them, whether anything should ever come back or not. Pass also the post-armistice loans out of the United States Treasury, which were for cleaning up the wreck in Europe. These constitute the war debts for which now we are hated in Europe and which no doubt will turn out to be worth very little. If the United States Treasury went to Wall Street to sell the long-term bonds it took from the Allies in place of their promissory notes, it would be lucky to get twenty cents on the dollar for them.

So consider only the private debt—that is, the American credit delivered to Europe since the war by American banks and American investors. All the terms were financial. The character of finance is selfish. Therefore, as to this private debt, representing five or six billions of American credit poured into Europe during the last eight years, it is permitted to ask: What have we gained thereby?

Definitely, in the first place, not the friendship or good will of Europe. On the contrary, we have raised against ourselves in Europe an ugly debtor mentality. This, you may say, is inevitable in the shape of human nature; creditors must expect it and allow for it. But what makes it much worse in Europe and gives it a sinister political importance is the prejudiced manner in which it is exploited, not only by the press and the politicians, but by responsible statesmen, by finance ministers who cannot balance their budgets, by governments when it is necessary to increase taxes.

Germany tells her people that if they did not have to pay reparations—called tribute—to the once allied nations, German wages would go up, German taxes would come down, German poverty would vanish, the German sun would rise.

The once allied nations say to Germany they are sorry; if they did not have to pay their war debts to the United States Treasury they could forego reparations, or in any case a great part of them, perhaps as much as two thirds. Yet all the time they keep saying to their own people that their troubles are multiplied upon them by the necessity to remit enormous sums each year to the United States Treasury on account of their war debts. That they collect these sums first from Germany as reparations is not emphasized. And the fact that so far there has been no payment of either reparations or war debts but with the aid of American credit does not interest them at all.

American loans to Germany have enabled her to pay reparations. Out of reparations from Germany the others make their annual payments on their war debts to the American Government. Anything we have yet got back from Europe was our own money, the worse for wear, and very little of that. But if you say this to a European, even to one who knows, he is offended. Very few of them do know, as a matter of fact; it is easier to believe what they hear from those who exploit the debtor mentality.

For a long time it was supposed that European feeling against America as the Shylock nation was owing to the nature of the debt—that it was a war debt and had a public character. Certainly there would be no such unreasonable feeling against a debt owing to private creditors. So we said, and saying it we continued to lend American credit in Europe until the weight of the private debt exceeded that of the war debt. Owing to its sheer magnitude this private debt now begins to assume a public character, and as it does there begins to rise about it and against it the same excitable popular feeling. Why are Americans so rich? Where do they get all this credit? Do they mean to enslave the world with their gold?

This is the sequel international finance does not foresee. When it comes suddenly to the end of its own resources, as it did in 1931, it must call on governments to interfere; after that all talk of keeping finance free of politics is sheer nonsense.

The real crisis in Germany last summer came after all nations had been relieved of war debts for one year, under the first Hoover plan. It was concerning the solvency of Germany in respect of her debt to private creditors that a seven-power conference of prime ministers was held in London in July. There the United States was represented by the American Secretary of State and the American Secretary of the Treasury, and there came forth the second Hoover plan, to save Germany from having to default on her debt, not to other governments, but to private creditors. The situation had got beyond the control of international finance; therefore, governments were obliged to interfere.

Again, later, when the British had to change their government in order to borrow American credit to save the Bank of England, a financial transaction with private creditors assumed a public character. The British Government borrowed the money, not from the American Government, but from American bankers. Nevertheless, because the American bankers had stipulated for public expenditures to be reduced in England and for the British budget to be balanced, it was possible, even plausible, for the

British Labor Party to say the Americans had exerted their colossal money power to destroy the Labor Government of Great Britain; and there are hundreds of thousands of unemployed in England who will think American bankers responsible for their diminished weekly dole out of the British public funds.

A private international debt is easily defined; it represents borrowing by private persons in one country from private persons in another. So also is a public international debt easily defined; it is a debt owed by one government to another. But debt may be private on one side and public on the other, as when the government of one nation borrows from private lenders in another. But let it be strictly a private debt, owing by the nationals of one country to the nationals of another, and yet if it becomes so large as to endanger the solvency and economic freedom of the debtor people, or so large as to alter their economic relations adversely, it will clothe itself with a public character and political consequences are bound to follow.

Our loans to Europe are of all kinds. They represent borrowing by European governments from the American Government, they represent borrowing by private persons and private organizations in Europe from private American lenders, and they represent borrowing by European governments and States and municipalities from private American creditors. Less and less do these distinctions matter, because more and more the character of an American loan is merely that particular aspect of one great body of debt. The political implications of it simply as debt take us unawares.

In the September, 1931, number of the *Revue des Deux Mondes,* M. Henri Bérenger, formerly French Ambassador to the United States and co-author of the Mellon-Bérenger war-debt funding agreement between France and the American Government, has an essay in the fine style of French logic on what has happened to the foreign policy of these Americans. For 145 years they had founded their foreign policy on Washington's farewell address to the American Congress. The words were few. No foreign entanglements. Woodrow Wilson was the first president to preach another doctrine, and the Americans rejected both him and his doctrine, and thereafter they sent only official observers to sit in the councils of Europe. "Then," says M. Bérenger, "President Hoover issues his messages to the world and sends his Secretary of the Treasury and his Secretary of State to negotiate with European ministers. This came after the launching of the presidential message of June 20, which to all intents and purposes was a message of entanglement. What has taken place on the other side of the Atlantic to make such derogation of the Washington doctrine possible, even popular?"

He answers his own question, saying: "For seven years American bankers have been engaged in entangling the United States with Europe. . . . Indeed, the network of steel and gold that America has cast upon Europe has been so powerful that it has become jammed of its own weight. A crash in Berlin is immediately felt in Washington and every panic in Frankfort causes trembling in Wall Street. When the crisis becomes worse and extends itself to the City of London the United States is so entangled that it is in danger of being strangled."

The French see it. In less than ten years finance has accomplished a fact the idea of which had been rejected by the American people for a century and a half, namely, the fact of foreign entanglement.

Since our lending to Europe bears us no friendship, only more and more dislike, and since it has caught us in a net of foreign entanglements contrary to our native wisdom, the question returns unanswered. What do we get out of it?

Now the voice of foreign commerce, saying: "But our lending abroad did increase our export trade. Our loans to Europe enabled her to buy from us great quantities of goods that otherwise she had been unable to buy. This kept our factories going, it kept our own labor employed."

And it is so, it did for a while. There is probably no point beyond which your export trade cannot be still further inflated so long as you lend people the money with which to buy your goods. But if it is good business when, having loaned your foreign customers the money to buy with, the goods are no sooner gone than you begin to wonder if you will get anything back, unless again you lend them the money to pay you with or forgive what they already owe—if that is business at all, then common sense is daftness and international finance has in itself the secret of wisdom.

Another voice is heard, saying: "But remember, this modern world is all one place. No nation may enjoy separate prosperity, not even this one. A war-haggard Europe was properly the concern of a country that had resources to spare. . . . That was reason enough for putting American credit at the command of Europe. Besides that it was our duty to do it, we should have been intelligent to do it on the ground of enlightened selfishness."

This high and excellent thought belongs to a harmony the world is not ready to play. There is first the probability that it will be embraced from opposite sides differently, by the lenders with one enthusiasm and by the borrowers with another, and that the transactions between them will not be governed by the simple rules of prudence, judgment and moral responsibility. When, moreover, you talk of lending as a duty, what do you mean? And how afterward shall you treat the contract? There is the further danger that the thought will be degraded to the saying that a rich nation, only because it is richer than others, is obliged to disperse its surplus among the envious and less fortunate. That idea, indeed, has been asserted by many European doctors of political economy, who either do not see or care not that international borrowing tends thereby to become reckless and irresponsible, and is soon tinged with the ancient thought of plunder.

THE RESCUE OF GERMANY

(THE GREAT AUGUST CRISIS)

The war has lasted sixteen years.

German guilt was a lie.

The Treaty of Versailles is the great crime of modern history.

Reparations are tribute.

In 1917 America joined the Allies against Germany because then her money was on that side.

Among nations, the debtor is dear to the creditor.

The Hoover debt holiday plan in 1931 was to protect two billions of American money in Germany, for now America is bound by what Germany owes her to be Germany's political friend.

—SELECTIONS FROM CURRENT GERMAN SAYINGS

Again, for the third time, Germany was threatening to sink in the sea of insolvency with all her creditors on board; again it was the creditors who frantically worked at the pumps. Their anxiety was greater than Germany's own. Why? For the singular reason that in this sea only creditors can drown.

If Germany sinks she will rise again, lightened by the loss of her creditors. Twice the creditors, unable otherwise to keep her afloat, have cast overboard great parcels of debt, and that at first was easy to do because the debt was political. The name of it was reparations. But now, in this third crisis, there are two kinds of debt and two kinds of creditors on board, all in the same dilemma. There is what survives of the original reparations debt, and there is now, besides, an enormous private debt, owing not by the German Government to other governments, but owing by the German Government, by all the German States, by German municipalities, by German banks, by German industry, to private lenders all over the world. This is new debt, created in the last six or seven years. The amount of it is nearly four billions of dollars. Roughly two thirds of it is owing to American banks, American investors, American lenders.

One value of this great private debt to Germany is that she can play it against the political debt.

As she watches her creditors working at the pumps she keeps saying: "Throw over the rest of the reparations debt. That is what is sinking us. Cast that away and the rest will float."

Then to her private creditors alone she says: "Don't you see how you can save yourselves? Only side with us and we will get rid of the reparations debt entirely. We tell you the rest will float."

This suggestion tends to divide the creditors and they begin quarreling among themselves. But they cannot be sure that if the reparations debt be jettisoned the rest will float. They are not sure of anything about Germany. So, in frustration, they appoint an international committee of experts to examine the ship from both the German point of view and that of the creditors, to reconcile them, and to say what burden of debt the ship can afford to bear, Germany willing.

The first international committee of experts had to work in a diving bell. Germany then, in 1924, was totally submerged. By inflating her money until it was worthless she had committed an act of complete national insolvency, internal and external. Nothing like it had ever happened before. Nevertheless, the experts found the ship itself to be quite sound and so reported. All that was necessary was to float it again on a tide of confidence. Once afloat it could bear a reparations debt burden of $625,000,000 a year.

That was the Dawes Plan; and on the undertaking to make it work the German Government borrowed $200,-000,000 gold from Great Britain, France and the United States, to begin a policy of fulfillment. Then immediately Germany at large launched herself upon a career of borrowing so amazing and reckless as to correspond to nothing that had ever happened before in the history of international finance, except, by contrast, her preceding career in bankruptcy by inflation. And this was the beginning of the private debt.

Five years later the Dawes Plan was sinking the ship. The sum of $625,000,000 a year was a disastrous thing in itself; but what made it very much worse was that the Dawes Plan did not say for how many years this burden should be carried. It had not fixed the total amount of reparations to be paid, only the annual payment on account. Unless the creditors would agree to fix a total, so that Germany might at least see the end of reparations, there was nothing for her to do but to embrace despair and sink again.

Then a second committee of international experts made an analysis of her resources and said she could afford to pay only $400,000,000 a year. That was the Young Plan; and on the undertaking to make that plan work, the German Government borrowed $300,000,000 from Great Britain, France and the United States, to launch a second policy of fulfillment.

But before the Young Plan had begun to work, the former head of the German Reichsbank and other Germans were going up and down in the world proclaiming the authentic propaganda that reparations still were bringing Germany to ruin; that unless she was relieved of that burden she would surely sink, and that if a second act of national insolvency, such as preceded the Dawes Plan, was the only way of escape, then this, with all its terrors, might come to seem the lesser German sacrifice.

It is weird to remember that with this propaganda running higher and higher, still Germany could continue to borrow abroad on a scale hitherto unheard of. American investors went on buying German bonds because the rate of interest was high; American banks went on putting their surplus funds on deposit in German banks for the same reason. They all said: "Oh, that is political propaganda about reparations. It has nothing to do with private finance or private investments." Nobody could imagine that the Germans would attack their own credit and really mean it; or that a second act of national bankruptcy was possible. It was a little like the warning on the sinking of the *Lusitania*. There it was, cold and authentic, and nobody believed it.

Suddenly in June, 1931, the lesser sacrifice did nevertheless become imminent. Germany was at the brink of national insolvency and calling on her creditors to forbear and save her from that disaster. Her inflated financial structure was about to fall. The Reichsbank was about to shut up. In that case, naturally, she would be obliged to default on the whole of her foreign debt, both political and private; and the private debt, owing not to governments but to foreign investors and foreign banks, had reached the prodigious total of nearly four billions of dollars. Could international finance afford to let such a thing happen? Were not Germany's creditors obliged in their own interest to come to her rescue?

The most sympathetic of Germany's creditors was Great Britain, not because she had more to lose than any other country—she had much less in jeopardy than the United States—but for other and complicated reasons. Every day in June the head of the Bank of England had New York on the telephone to tell American bankers how desperate the German situation was, how daily it grew worse, and why it behooved the United States to take great measures. Only the United States had the resources to save Germany. England alone was helpless to avert the calamity. France was obscure. The United States was obliged in its own interest to act. For suppose Germany failed. What would happen to American banks with enormous sums on deposit in German banks? And what would happen to the German bonds that had been sold to banks and private investors all over the United States? What would happen to American banks that had those German bonds in their investment reserves? When the head of the Bank of England was not calling New York, the British Government itself was calling Washington and saying the same things.

Such were the circumstances under which President Hoover proposed an international debt holiday. No reparations to be collected by the former Allies from Germany, no payments to be made by Europe on account of war debts to the United States Treasury, for a period of one year. The effect of this was a loan of $400,000,000 to Germany. That was the amount she would have had otherwise to pay away on account of reparations. And besides that effect, international finance at the same time made a direct loan of $100,000,000 to the German Reichsbank to meet any emergency. The money was provided by the Federal Reserve Bank of New York, the Bank of England and the Bank of France. On this day's work international finance heaved a great sigh. Nothing less than the bankruptcy of Germany had been averted. For several days there was a wonderful rise in German bonds, in securities of all kinds, even in commodities, the whole world over.

What followed immediately was a headlong flight from the German mark. Private banks in England, France, Holland, Switzerland and the United States that had been keeping money in German banks because the rate of interest was high were, on second thought, more anxious than ever to call their deposits home, for after all, a year was a short time and nobody knew what would happen at the end of the holiday.

But that was not all. The Germans themselves were in

flight from the mark. They had been stealing away from it quietly for a year or more; now they began to run. They took German marks to the Reichsbank and bought dollars in New York, pounds sterling in London, French francs in Paris. This could be done through the mechanism of foreign exchange; and when they had exchanged their marks at the Reichsbank for dollars payable in New York, pounds sterling payable in London and French francs payable in Paris, they had then only to wire to New York, to London and to Paris to keep their dollars, their pounds sterling and their francs on deposit. Germans who knew not how to convert German marks into foreign bank deposits through the mechanism of foreign exchange found simple ways to get rid of them. For example, they would go to the nearest border and tender the largest possible German mark bill for a small railroad ticket, wanting not the little journey into a foreign country but the change in Dutch guilders or Swiss francs, for hoarding.

The Hoover debt holiday plan took effect on June 30, and Germany on that date, with $400,000,000 less to pay out and $100,000,000 new credit borrowed at the same time, was half a billion dollars to the good. Nevertheless, within ten days Doctor Luther, head of the German Reichsbank, was going about Europe in an airplane, to Basle, to Paris, to London, saying Germany must have immediately the loan of half a billion dollars more. The whole benefit of the Hoover debt holiday plan had been swallowed up in the flight from the German mark, and Germany's financial plight was much worse than before. The lesser German sacrifice, that is to say, the bankruptcy of Germany, now was really imminent.

International finance was horrified. Where was the end of this? The Germans rushing their own money out of Germany and Germany at the same time imploring her creditors to put more in, to save her and to save themselves!

"It is a sieve," said the French. "A perfect sieve. Moreover, it is very probably a trap. Does Germany think that by threatening to repudiate her debts she can oblige her creditors to go on putting more and more in, merely in order to get a fixed amount out?"

The French were in a very strong position—much stronger than the English. The Bank of England had been steadily losing gold for a long time and was greatly worried about it, whereas the Bank of France had the second largest gold fund in the world and was steadily increasing it. The French knew very well that the idea of another great international loan to Germany would fail if they declined to support it. So they said: "Very well. We will consider taking part in another international loan to Germany provided the Germans will behave as debtors should. Debtors ought not to be cultivating a military spirit toward their creditors. Therefore, let the Germans disband their Steel Helmets, which represent the old military spirit again. Let them stop spending their creditors' money for what they call pocket battleships, which are really very formidable sea weapons. Let them undo their bargain of union with Austria, which is contrary to the Treaty of Versailles."

At this Doctor Luther flew home to Berlin. He represented only the German Reichsbank, and nothing else of the German Government; he was therefore not competent to discuss political matters.

On his return a song of bitterness burst in Germany. The war still! The French again! They would take advantage of Germany's desperate necessities to make humiliating political demands. Having ruined the Hoover plan by making difficulties about it until the grand effect was lost, now they would use their financial strength to force Germany into economic slavery.

The English, dreading more than any other nation a crash of the financial structure of Europe, spilled unction on these waters. They proposed a conference of prime

ministers to be held in London and persuaded the German
Chancellor to come by way of Paris and stop there in his
best German manner for such impression as it might make
on the implacable French nature. The German Chancellor
did, taking with him his foreign minister and a body of
eminent experts. The French received them at the railway station under an arch of flowers. Any one who even
a little understands the French would know what that
meant. It meant that the French were in a logical mood
and that when the embracings were over they would find
themselves astronomically removed from any point of
view but their own. And so it was.

Yet what the Germans were saying was enough to make
the blood of international finance run cold. They were
saying that Germany had no plan of her own to propose.
She had only the facts to present. It was up to her creditors to regard the facts and then decide whether to save
Germany in order to save themselves. The Germans
said they were talking not only of their political debt,
that is to say, reparations, on account of which they
were obliged to find $400,000,000 a year; they were think-
ing even more of Germany's new private debt, amounting now to nearly four billions of dollars. This was
money Germany and her nationals had borrowed during
six years on their bonds and notes and short-dated
I. O. U.'s from banks and from private investors in
America, England, France, Holland, Switzerland, Scan-
dinavia and elsewhere, and more from Americans than
from any of the others. A great deal of it had been what
is called short-term credit, that is to say, loans for short
periods such as may be renewed again and again if the
sky stays blue and yet such as may be suddenly called
away at the first sign of bad weather. It had been
dangerous to borrow so much short-term credit. They
said they knew that all the time. Much of this short-
term credit has been unwisely, some of it extravagantly,
spent; they knew that also. Admitted it as a fact. Never-

theless, it was necessary to face the facts. Now many of those who had been lending Germany this money were calling for it back. But having spent it, how could Germany give it back, or, in any case, all at once? It was due and payable—yes. The creditors were within their rights to call for it back. But they were calling to the vast deep of ten thousand empty German tills. If they insisted, there was only one thing for Germany to do. That was to confess herself bankrupt and so treat all creditors alike. It was not Germany's problem really. It was a problem for international finance to solve. The only way for the creditors to get interest or principal out of Germany, or reparations either, was to go on lending her the money to pay them.

At this point of the German discourse international finance began to shudder. For six years it had been pouring money into the German treasury, into German industry, into German banks, saying all the time: "If the world expects Germany to pay reparations it must lend her enormous sums of capital to build up her internal economy." Now Germany saying to her creditors: "If you expect to be paid you must lend us the money to pay you with. To save your investments you must save Germany first."

And what is it Germany must be saved from? First and always from reparations.

But the Germans were not through. They went on to say that unless international finance came to Germany's rescue with an enormous new loan it might expect, first, a total eclipse of German solvency toward the outside world. After that, what? After that, communism—a red Germany, for what that would mean to the peace and comfort of her neighbors. And suppose this did not happen. Suppose for her own sake she could avoid going red in a political sense. Nevertheless, if now it becomes necessary for Germany to save herself with no more benefit of credit, she will be obliged to go red in an economic sense. She knows how to save herself. She has only to forget her creditors, forget the rules of capital, forget the arrangements by means of which international finance has been trying to support a high capital structure, and simply flood the markets of the world with unlimited quantities of cheap German goods.

So that was what the conference of prime ministers had to face in London.

First, in the obvious aspect, a sinking Germany—sinking for want of an international loan to keep herself afloat. An international loan would be normally the business of international bankers on its merits. But international finance at this time was practically unconscious. Germany had created a situation quite beyond its resources, its experience or its imagination. International finance is not a bank, not a gold hoard; it is a mechanism. It would be willing enough to take German bonds for half a billion more—if the bonds could be sold. But where could any more German bonds be sold? The world was already full of them, all selling at a terrible discount, because so many holders were trying to get rid of them. International finance, in short, was out of ideas. Possibly the prime ministers with all their heads together could think of something. Anyhow, that was the only hope; that was what the conference was for.

The conference took place in London in the third week of July. The seven principal powers of the world were represented. Six of them were anxious creditors; the seventh was the astonishing debtor. The United States was represented by Mr. Stimson, Secretary of State, and by Mr. Mellon, Secretary of the Treasury.

Regard it. In weight and size and shape it is the most august meeting of high statesmen since war time. Imagine the opening, the formal gestures, a speech by the British premier saying now every one must forget his own and think only of the whole, of what will be best to do for the good of the world, since only by unselfish

international collaboration can they hope to solve the
problem before them.

Suppose Germany shall speak next. Has she any plan
of her own to propose?

No. Germany is helpless. She has no plan. She sub-
mits the facts and leaves the solution to her creditors.
All she can think of is that an international loan of half
a billion dollars will keep her afloat.

For how long?

That she cannot say. For a while at least. It would
mean a breathing space.

What has Germany to offer for such a loan?

Nothing. Germany is helpless. She has nothing left
to offer.

But what security?

None, except her promise to pay.

But her promises to pay already exceed her power of
performance. Is not that the very problem?

That, of course, is the problem. The Germans admit it
simply.

Will Germany be willing to secure such a loan by a
lien on her customs receipts, as the French have suggested?

No.

Why not?

Because the German people will not submit to that
humiliation. They will destroy any government that dares
to propose it.

Will Germany make any political concessions to appease the French, such as to stop building battleships and
to disband the troublesome Steel Helmets?

No.

Why not?

Again, because the German people will not suffer
that humiliation. They would sooner go red.

But perhaps Germany will agree to stop working for a
revision of the treaties? Perhaps she will agree, when

this crisis is over, to return to the Young Plan and observe it faithfully, instead of trying meantime to get it revised?

Certainly not. Germany would tactfully remind her very distinguished collaborators that what they are dealing with is a financial crisis. It is a mistake, not to say a breach of concord, to load it with political difficulties.

Very well. But with nothing to yield, nothing to give, nothing to offer that has not already been twice exhausted, on what ground does Germany expect her creditors to lend her another half billion of dollars?

The answer is ready. Germany would think her creditors could see the importance of doing it on the ground of their own interest. Suppose they refuse. Suppose they let Germany go. In the first place, the financial consequences will be uncontrollable. They cannot be confined to Germany alone. Germany might have to sink, but her creditors would sink with her, and the effect might well be a world-wide financial crash. Secondly, that would be the end of responsible government in Germany. Suppose then nationalism were to rise in its extreme form, or else communism. In any case Germany would be obliged to save herself, even though to do so it were necessary to repudiate not only her debts but all other forms of economic restraint, cut wages, cut prices, and overwhelm the markets of the world with German goods.

Helpless Germany! Able to challenge her creditors. Able to threaten the political structure of Europe. Able to threaten the economic structure of the world. How had she arrived at this oblique eminence? By intending her mind to it? By taking advantage of the stupidity of the world? By drift of forces that happened to be working for her? And was threaten the right word? No member of the London conference, gazing at the Germans, could answer even the last of these questions.

The English were deeply agitated at the thought of

Germany going economically red, much more than at the thought of political Bolshevism. A Royal Commission had just produced a mighty treatise on the necessity to restore the world's price level. Its conclusion was that to stabilize prices at the fallen level would be a calamity. Prices at whatever cost or risk, even if necessary by a process of scientific international inflation, must be stabilized on a higher level, or else a great deal of the world's capital representing what formerly had been a normal expectation of profit, would be forever lost. Dumping, therefore—the thought or word of it—filled the British mind with dismay. Russian dumping was terror enough. A campaign of propaganda to bar Russian goods from English markets was at that moment running in the London press. But how much more formidable would Germany be in that red economic rôle, with her skill, her experience, her long ambition to dominate the foreign markets of the world, and her powerful industrial machine—the most powerful and efficient in Europe! And how politely the Germans were saying it!

Yet there was no misunderstanding what they meant; moreover, the idea was rising in Germany. The German newspapers were saying that an economic policy of self-saving, with no further benefit of international finance, would have the advantage to "loosen political and financial bonds which were not unconditionally necessary and have hitherto acted only as brakes on our development." And saying this at a time when the German Government held the German press in strict censorship.

The English could imagine those mountains of coal visible at the German pit heads breaking over Europe and running down into Italy, to the ruin of the British coal trade; they could see German manufactures underselling British goods everywhere in foreign markets. The British press touched the subject in a very guarded manner, hardly at all. But the *London Times* said it was understood that Mr. Ramsay MacDonald had taken the Germans aside and said to them that a policy of German dumping would bring them into conflict with England. He said England would retaliate, perhaps with no idea whatever in his head of how really it could.

Well, the mighty seven-power conference of six anxious creditors and one astonishing debtor failed to find a magic chemistry. It labored and brought forth two suggestions, then adjourned, pronouncing its own benediction. The suggestions were these: First, that since a new international loan to Germany was not immediately feasible, each of the six creditor governments should recommend to its bankers to leave in Germany the remainder of their deposits instead of calling them home. Second, that a third committee of international experts be called up to study Germany's situation, analyze her necessities, and report.

It sounds very little. From the creditors' point of view it was less than nothing. And yet Germany, with nothing to yield, nothing to give, nothing to offer, had won three major points.

First, she got her loan, though it was involuntary on the part of the lenders. When the principal American and English banks, together with such others as could be bullied or persuaded, agreed to leave their overdue deposits and short-term credits in the German banks, instead of calling them home, that was the equivalent of a loan of more than three quarters of a billion dollars to Germany. She had the money; she could continue to use it. It had simply been reloaned to her.

Secondly, Germany gained a third international committee of experts to protect her from her creditors; and the American member of this committee was Albert H. Wiggin, head of the Chase National Bank in New York, publicly committed to the proposition that reparations and war debts should be heavily scaled down or cancelled altogether, and that at the same time American tariffs should be reduced in order that Europe might sell more of its goods in American markets.

Thirdly, what Germany most wanted was to hang a mourning wreath upside down on the Young Plan, and that she did.

What the third international committee of experts represented was perhaps the last decline of the make-believe that there could ever be an economic approach to the problem of German reparations. How can there be, when the German Government itself officially speaks of reparations as tribute? People who believe reparations are tribute—and the Germans do deeply believe it—will not behave as if reparations were debt. Yet that is how the world has been expecting the Germans to behave. Nor can there be any purely economic solutions with Germany, private or other, so long as Germans keep thinking, "This is the sixteenth—" or, "This is the seventeenth year of the war." Her principal creditors, remember, were her enemies in the war.

It is easy enough to make an economic analysis of the 1931 financial crisis in Germany. That can be done in one sentence. The great German machine, having been raised on borrowed capital to be the most powerful and the most efficient in Europe, was running on borrowed gas. Given that fact, any one would know what the consequences were bound to be. But what is the fact worth? Why was the German machine running on borrowed gas? Why were the Germans putting their own gas out of Germany for safe keeping, in the banks of foreign countries, and borrowing gas, that is to say, short-term credit, from other people? Why?

When in early July the head of the German Reichsbank was going about Europe in an airplane, soliciting an international loan of half a billion dollars (gas) to keep the German machine from stalling, to save Germany from bankruptcy—at that time the Germans' own estimate of the amount of German money (gas again) on deposit in New York, London, Paris, Amsterdam and other foreign money centers was a billion dollars. There was so much German money on deposit in Paris alone that if it had been called for all in one day the French money market would have been demoralized. There was no danger of its being called for. The Germans did not want their own money; they wanted other people's money.

These you may state as economic facts, bearing on the German crisis. They explain the crisis. Yet they are not themselves to be explained in economic terms. If the Germans had kept their own money at home there need not have been a financial crisis. They had enough gas of their own to keep their machine going. But they preferred to hoard their own in foreign countries. Seeing all this clearly, the French were unable to take a strictly financial view of the German crisis. They kept asking: "Why have the Germans brought this condition upon themselves?" Certainly not for economic reasons.

And remember that all this time the reparations debt has been not an economic burden, not a financial burden, but a mental burden only. Actual burden it never was, for the simple reason that never yet has Germany paid any reparations. She has made the world pay them for her; she has made her creditors pay themselves.

In the beginning she had resort to the naïve expedient of simply printing paper marks and selling them all over the world so long as anybody would buy them. And people did buy them in prodigious quantities. The lower they fell the more they bought, saying all the time, "Germany will never repudiate her money; it is unimaginable," and thinking, therefore, it was a fine speculation to buy marks. The buyers of these marks, which were going to be repudiated, and the holders of German bonds receiving interest in those same marks—they paid the first reparations, not Germany. Germany took their money in exchange for her paper marks and handed it over to her creditors. When at last the cost of printing and shipping paper marks in bundles was more than the marks would bring, Germany stopped her printing presses, stopped paying reparations, and announced her total insolvency.

Then the French conceived the grim idea of collecting reparations by force. That was when they went into the Ruhr and seized the very heart of Germany's industrial machine. All they proved was that you cannot collect reparations from an unwilling people by force. The Germans would not work their machine to produce tribute for the French. There were strikes and riots and, worse still, threat of wrecking the machine itself or jamming it by sabotage. Imagine it, when the slip of a monkey wrench in the hands of a sullen German workman might cost the French a million francs of tribute. That was the French problem in the Ruhr, where they had the industrial heart of Germany in their hands. Suppose they had said: "Very well, we shall take the machine into our own hands and run it." But that would mean bringing workers and technicians from their own country. There would be no profit in that. Besides, if they did it, they would have a starving, idle German population on their hands. The Ruhr party cost the French more than they got out of it. No reparations that way.

At this impasse the nations of Europe joined to call on the United States, saying: "We are emotionally and politically mad. We have only sanity enough left among us to know that we are. Simply, we cannot think economically. You over there have the vision of distance. Think of a way in which we may go on here in Europe. For unless you can we shall go to pieces. Bring us a plan." We did. We sent American experts to straighten them out; we gave them the Dawes Plan. Germany accepted it, crossed her heart for a policy of fulfillment, and borrowed $200,000,000 gold to get started with.

Since the Dawes Plan took effect—since 1924, that is to say—Germany's net payments on account of reparations, according to her own figures, have amounted to $2,350,000,000.

In the same time, still according to her own statistics, she has borrowed from other countries the incredible sum of $3,750,000,000.

This is to say, that since 1924 she has borrowed $1,400,000,000 more than she has paid out on account of reparations.

Roughly, two thirds of this borrowed money came from the United States. The next largest part of it came from Great Britain. The rest of it from France, Holland, Switzerland, and other lending countries. More than three quarters of the total came from her former enemies.

Simply to say that Germany borrowed with one hand and paid reparations with the other, or that out of every dollar she borrowed she paid sixty-three cents in reparations and kept thirty-seven, does not tell the whole story. The money had a circular movement. It went one way into Germany, stopped there for ninety days, six months, a year or more, to work, and then went out another way, like water turning a mill wheel. It is important to remember this, for it explains many otherwise incomprehensible effects. The money did not just go in and out again; it was detained and put to work. That is what people who talk economics mean when they say that with borrowed money Germany built up her internal economy in order to be able to pay reparations and then paid them out of the increase of her wealth. She did build up her internal economy amazingly. She knew how to bend that stream of money on the wheel. And that is how it happens that she is to-day the second most powerful industrial nation in the world. The United States is first in the world. Germany is first in Europe.

She spent the borrowed money under three heads, namely: *One,* for housing of all kinds; *two,* on her industrial machine, to rebuild it, rationalize it, increase its power; and, *three,* for public works such as parks, baths, civic and recreation centers, schools, stadiums, exposition buildings, new city halls, new post offices, roads, even monuments.

A passion to build possessed them. Under the head of housing they completed in the one year 1930 more than

300,000 habitations. The great weight of new housing was for wage workers, state servants and people of moderate means. Any new housing project in the mass principle is called a settlement. So, workers' settlements, railway employees' settlements, post-office employees' settlements, bachelors' settlements. But settlements also in selected places for the well-to-do. What we should call real estate developments on a very large scale. The aggregate is prodigious. The only way to see it really is from the air because one settlement or one series of flat dwellings may be the size of a town. Moreover, you would have to drive an endless distance to see it from the ground. It is in character extensive and in new places. The cities have not been rebuilt. They have not changed much. These people do not tear down old things to build new ones. For new things new ground. All this change is in the environs.

The building passion overflowed necessity, became extravagant, experimental, sportive. New time, new materials, new shapes, new measures, new intentions. Churches all of steel and glass. The modernistic extreme in villas, morgues, hotels, schools, skyscrapers, commercial buildings. It was an architect's festival.

Many creditors are scandalized by the signs of Germany's extravagance with borrowed money, the French and the English more than Americans, since they have less understanding of extravagance in principle. The Germans admit it. They may say truthfully that they have been heard to denounce it themselves, to one another. All the same, they went on with it. And then, too, great sums were purposefully spent for the future, as for a new fourth bridge across the Rhine at Cologne, now one of the engineering marvels of Europe.

The French said: "There is no present necessity for this bridge. Why do you build it? You do not pay reparations with a bridge."

The Germans said: "We shall sometime need it, and we build it now to keep our people employed."

It was their instinct, or their wisdom, to increase their power and improve their conditions by any means possible, even though it was with creditors' money they did it. And from their own point of view they were right. What they have built they will continue to possess. Gold they may lose; credit they may lose. But machines, factories, power plants, bridges, public buildings, roads, laboratories, better dwellings, parks—these things remain. They cannot fly away. What happens to the money seems relatively unimportant. Money is not things. It is merely the token of things. Destroy the token and there are the things still, physically untouched by a financial crisis. You can invent new tokens to represent them. That has happened before. Less than ten years ago was not German money wholly destroyed? The things it had represented, they were not destroyed, not even German credit, which was an intangible thing. A new money token was invented in place of the one that had been destroyed, and lo! Germany was in good credit again, the whole world anxious to become her creditor.

Moreover, by what may seem to have been reckless and extravagant use of borrowed money, Germany has created a great body of social wealth, visible as fine housing, recreational facilities and other means to human well-being, the existence of which tends to defeat what impulse there may have been to communism. If there was any real danger of communism in Germany, which is doubtful, it is greatly lessened by the fact that the German wage workers have much more comfort, well-being and freedom of ego to defend than ever before.

The red menace in all political senses is probably seven tenths conjuration.[1] The communists are four or five million all together. But they have no leadership. There is not one important mind among them. There is an idea in Germany that the rulers of Soviet Russia do not want Ger-

[1] Since this was written Von Hindenburg has been reëlected president of the German republic.

many to go red—at least not yet. They are too fearful of the effect it might have on her efficiency and productive power and too anxious for the present to draw upon that efficiency and power for their own needs. Whether this is true or not, the Russians would be very intelligent to take that view and to maintain in Germany merely a tin façade of communism, numerically strong, politically weak.

The well-poised German's view of communism is first of all cynical. He says: "It is something to have in the hand." He means that when the German Government is having difficulties with the Reichstag it can rally supporters by waving the red menace or threatening to take support from the communists; and that when German statesmen are dealing with the outside world, as at the London conference, they can say: "Responsible government has its back to the wall in Germany. Uphold us for your own sake as much as for ours, for if this government falls we shall all of us have to face communism in Germany." And it works. It has been working ever since the armistice.

None but a German can understand the involutions of German politics, and there is reason to doubt that a German does. Parties beginning at the center and shading right and left, parties within parties, parties left of the right and parties right of the left, all in a ceaseless way of quarreling, not about ideas as such but about the philosophy and theory of ideas. Any new idea has first to be examined from the point of view of party advantage, and then, if ever, on its merits. As you look at this ill-natured, monotonous eddy of grumbling disagreement, their whole political-mindedness apparently revolving in muddy innocence of realities, you will say it is hopeless, worse than drifting. How can there be a sense of direction among them? But then when you look at what lies behind them in the last ten years and at what they have done with their advantages against the world, you can almost imagine that a Machiavellian intelligence has been guiding them. Look again at the great eddy of political confusion and it may occur to you that here their disagreements cancel one another and all their passion for petty interference is absorbed, so that beyond it in the field of reality their true intelligence, their racial intuition, or whatever it is that leads them, is all the more free to act upon their destiny, without interference.

For example, during the July, 1931, crisis they passed from a republican form of government to a dictatorship and were hardly aware of it. The constitution was suspended in fact; they were governed by decree, their parliament was in a state of self-abnegation, employers were ordered to withhold fifty per cent. of wages due, scores of newspapers were shut up, a German could not cross the border without paying first a fine of twenty-five dollars, free comment touching the German Chancellor's work at London was "verboten" lest it interfere with the result—and there was no protest. Under the circumstances a dictatorship was necessary. It could set itself up automatically. No party was responsible for it; therefore, no party cared. And the interminable sounds issuing from the eddy were the same as before.

And if Germany did go red, in a political sense, it would not be like Russian communism. The Germans have not the heart to destroy their own things. They overthrew a monarchy and destroyed nothing. It never occurred to them to destroy its human symbol, namely, the Kaiser. He was exiled on a pension, partly to appease the world; he was unwept because he had failed. But the Crown Prince was received back and now is active in German politics, at the extreme right. Least of all would the Germans destroy their tools, that is to say, their own industrial power, for that is their first source of hope.

Yet notwithstanding the reduction of the red menace, if it was real, and notwithstanding the social improvement in Germany, which is very real, many creditors are still scandalized. They keep saying: "From the German point of view, yes; but it was borrowed money. They spent it for such things as even the lenders cannot always afford. They must have known as they were spending it that they would be unable to pay it back when it was due."

That is not exactly what they know. They probably thought very little about it; and, moreover, if they had thought about it they would not have cared. To understand this it will be necessary to go further with the German point of view.

To begin with, most of the money was coming from American lenders, and every German has it in his heart that his country was beaten by America, not by the Allies. But for the vast weight of American resources, first as they were loaned to the Allies and then as they went directly into the war, German victory had been inevitable, according to destiny. American money thwarted that destiny.

Then consider the emotional conviction under which now every process of the German mind takes place. How it was arrived at does not matter as a practical fact. The conviction is that there was a conspiracy to crush Germany. It did not succeed. Yet there will be no justice in the world until the Treaty of Versailles is destroyed; and the special infamy of that document is that it contains a confession of guilt extorted from a people reduced to their knees by the power of the whole world.

It follows that they have no sense of debt on account of reparations. Simply, reparations are tribute. It follows also that the secret German language about Germany's principal creditors may be extremely ironical, with some special emphasis toward Americans, from whom it was so easy to borrow money to pay tribute with. How could they be expected to care very much about what happened to the money they borrowed? It was the money of their enemies, and as they were borrowing and spending it to increase their power they were counting the years the war had lasted—fourteen, fifteen, sixteen. And what a stupid world of lenders!

The finality of all fact about the Germans is that they have the feelings, the mentality and the motives of an injured race. Their sense of injury is obsessional, so deep and so ugly as to seem a national psychosis, as it probably is. Germany against the world is the one thought that will unite them; and that never fails. Self-commiseration is their emotional habit.

They believe it themselves when they tell you Germany is poor. You must not be deceived by appearances. There is bitter distress just beneath the surface. There is no fat, or, if there is, then it is not good fat. Germany's tissues are white, if you could only see them. Reparations do that. She is helpless; she is at the mercy of her creditors. Her middle class has been destroyed. Can you destroy a middle class without suffering? People come to look. They see Germans eating and bathing and trying to be gay, but this is desperation, the behavior of a people living in fear of deluge. Really it is not so. They are not gay. If the shops are busy that is because they are afraid of their own money and spend it in order to hoard things instead. They remember inflation. And if they go out to dine once more in a good way, it is because they do not know what will happen to-morrow.

One who had heard this theme too much and heard it again from a group of tense, earnest Germans at dinner in Berlin last July, tried turning their minds around.

"I imagine myself to be a German," he said. "The year is 1924. I am gazing at the heavens. Do you remember that after the armistice, or, as other people say, after the war, there came a craze for heaven gazing in Germany? That is when you began to build these wonderful planetariums."

"Yes," they said, a little bewildered.

"I imagine I was a German in 1924," he continued, "at a planetarium, as every one else was, and as I sat gazing at the celestial mechanism, suddenly I saw the future of Germany, clearly, like a dream."

"What was it?" they asked. "What did you see?"

"Wait," he said. "First, do you remember what it was like in 1924? The enemy tarried in the Rhineland, holding it for hostage of good behavior. The French were in the Ruhr, squeezing the very heart of Germany. Foreign commissions were seated in Berlin, watching and minding everything. Germany was insolvent. Her money was worthless. A million marks would hardly buy a cold supper."

The Germans groaned.

"Then the vision," he said. "I imagine that as a German I saw what would happen to Germany in the next six years. I saw that in 1930 she would be free of foreign control, the enemy would be out of the Rhineland, the French would be out of the Ruhr. I saw that in 1930 Germany would be the best equipped nation in Europe, paramount in Europe for industrial power and second in the world only to the United States. I saw that in 1930 she would be the best housed nation in Europe, if not in the world. I saw that in 1930 her exports would pass Great Britain's for the first time, and this had been her life-long ambition. I saw that in 1930 she would hold the blue ribbon of the sea against England, with the two newest and fastest ships on the Atlantic, and that she would have once more a great merchant marine, all new and modern, besides building ships for other nations in successful competition with England's shipbuilding industry. I saw that in 1930 she would be first in aviation among European nations, with the largest land plane in the world, the largest sea plane in the world and the finest airports. I saw that in 1931 she would be strong enough to say 'no' to the French when as a condition for an international loan they proposed that Germany disband her weaponless army of Steel Helmets and stop building battleships. I saw one of the new ten-thousand-ton battleships and reflected on the folly of Germany's enemies. They thought to limit the strength of her sea weapons with a piece of writing, which says a German warship shall not exceed ten thousand tons. All they did was to stimulate German inventiveness, for under this limitation she had made a sea weapon in ten thousand tons that was probably equal to any 25,000-ton warship in the world. I saw that in 1931 she would be strong enough to dare say officially, 'Reparations are tribute,' which was notice that she was almost strong enough to repudiate them. And I saw that meanwhile, during six years, she had borrowed much more from her enemies than she had paid them as reparations, which meant that she herself had paid no reparations at all. I saw that in 1931 she would be strong enough, without weapons, to threaten the political peace of Europe and strong enough to threaten the economic rhythm of the world by letting loose the full power of her industries and laboratories. There the vision ended. I imagined I had been asleep. It was a dream. What a fabulous dream! And yet all of it has come true."

"It has come true," said the Germans, with not the slightest rift in their gloom. It was deeper than ever. "Such things as you mention are true," they said. "But you are not a German. You cannot imagine what it is like. The situation of Germany is desperate."

What were they thinking of then? Their lost colonies? The French empire? The new French fortifications? Their isolation? The guilt phrase in the Versailles Treaty? You will never know. It may be they were thinking how awkward it was for the stream of American money out of which they had been paying reparations to dry up suddenly. Unless it rises again they may have to decide whether actually to pay something by way of tribute or repudiate reparations before they are quite ready to risk it.

OPERATING THE GOLDEN GOOSE

(POST MORATORIUM)

"The Federal Reserve System has been threatened with raids upon its gold supply by foreign nations, notably by France. There has been that threatening situation, the conjecture—and it is a conjecture—being that that country wanted to affect our situation with respect to reparations and with respect to her indebtedness to the United States. I do not make the assertion. I say that it is conjecture. The officials of the Bank of France have simply outwitted the officials of the Federal Reserve System of this country."

> —SENATOR CARTER GLASS,
> Formerly Secretary of the Treasury, moving in the United States Senate, February 17, 1932, the Glass-Steagall bill, an emergency act to protect the American gold reserve.

To the further education of American credit abroad enter these autumnal sights and experiences, *videlicet:*

1. The gold honor of the American dollar impugned in Europe, where our lending of it had been so prodigal. Our credit impugned by our debtors! And for what reason? For the reason that we had been too free with it; precisely for the reason that our debtors knew they had borrowed too much on poor security.

2. The rationally impossible spectacle of debtor nations raiding the gold reserves of a creditor nation while the

creditor is self-bound and helpless under an agreement not to collect its debts from them.

3. The strange experience of a creditor nation finding itself beholden to one of its principal debtors, the debtor undertaking on grounds of generosity and helpfulness to stop raiding the creditor's gold reserves short of the point at which the creditor's own gold solvency might seem to be in jeopardy.

4. The sight of public ovations in this the creditor country to the premier of one of its principal debtors when he comes to tell us that more of Europe's war debts must be charged to the American taxpayer in a spirit of international friendship; more public ovations as he departs with our promise to consider it.

5. Experience of numbness and a sense of ill-being in the body of American credit, probably psychic.

And for all of this the narrative, beginning abruptly.

What with the American moratorium for a year on war debt payments owing to the United States Treasury, the relending of 700 or 800 millions of short-term American credit in Germany to save her from wretched default, a cash loan at the same time to the Reichsbank, then a cash loan to the Bank of England to save the gold honor of the pound sterling and immediately another to the British Treasury for the same purpose—with all of this we put no less than a billion and a half of American gold credit into Europe during the summer of 1931, thinking thereby to avert the disaster of a total financial collapse.

The specific intent of our loans to the Bank of England and to the British Treasury was to keep the mighty pound sterling on a gold basis—keep it, that is to say, at its full traditional gold value. This the British themselves were heroically resolved to do, for if the Bank of England should be unable to pay its notes in gold on demand that would mean repudiation, inflation, a depreciated British currency no longer worth its face in gold. It would mean, naturally, a terrific humiliation of British

credit over the whole world. Nevertheless, this was bound
to happen. There was no stopping the run on the Bank
of England. Its borrowing in New York was too desperate and only increased the alarm. This American gold
credit was like bundles of currency piled in the window
of a doomed bank to put the depositors off when it has
the opposite effect, because nobody believes it will be
enough. After the Bank of England had borrowed all
the American gold credit it could get on its own signa-
ture and two weeks after the British Treasury had itself
borrowed 200 million more in New York to save the
pound sterling, the Bank of England suspended gold
payments. The gold value of the pound sterling immediately declined one quarter and Great Britain was on a
paper money basis.

Now, with Great Britain off the gold basis, Germany
financially frozen, Austria and Hungary bankrupt, and
all war debt payments owing by Europe to the United
States Treasury suspended for a year, the situation was
simply this—that what Europe owed us she could either
pay in depreciated paper currency or need not pay at all,
whereas anything we owed or might owe to Europe was
payable in gold on demand, because the United States
was still on a gold basis.

To make it clear, suppose you have at your bank two
separate accounts. In one account you owe the bank a
million dollars on a long-term promissory note which you
have undertaken to pay off gradually with interest. The
other account is current. You have there a credit, say, of
fifty thousand dollars. That is the account in which you
transact your daily business. Now suppose you go to your
bank and say: "I cannot pay the interest on that million-
dollar note. I am bankrupt if you make me pay." Saying
this, you put yourself in the hands of the bank. It can
demand payment and sell you out, foreclose on your business, take all your property. But the bank does not want
to do that. It says: "All right. These are hard times.

Let the interest go for a year and let the note run." You say: "But how about my current account in which I have fifty thousand dollars? What will you do with that?" The bank says: "Well, of course you have to go on doing business. We will treat that account as if you were solvent. Go on drawing your checks against it as before and keep your business going. All of this will work out in time." Very good. It is a reasonable arrangement. But suppose the next day you walk into that bank and say: "I'm afraid of this institution. It's too loose with its credit. I'm afraid my current account is not safe. I am closing it out. Here is my check for fifty thousand dollars and I want it in gold, please."

That would be difficult behaviour on the part of a debtor, owing his bank a million dollars on which he is unable to pay the interest, yet demanding $50,000 in gold. Yet, strange as the fact is, having made this arrangement with him, the bank is obliged to pay him his credit balance of fifty thousand, and pay it in gold if he demands gold, or confess itself insolvent.

Between an individual and his bank such a case would be preposterous. Between Europe and this country it is in the same nature preposterous, though the fact may be somewhat obscured by its own magnitude and by the high language surrounding it.

Owing this country more than ten billions of dollars— less than half of it war debts, the rest of it representing private and public borrowing from American investors and American banks—Europe nevertheless had very large credit balances here, payable on demand. You might put the sum of them at one billion. These balances had originated in various ways. While American banks had been putting deposits in European banks, especially German banks, because the rate of interest was high, European banks at the same time had been putting deposits in American banks for an opposite reason. They wanted safety. So there were credit balances of that character, payable to Europe on demand. Then European exporters had been in the habit of leaving their profits on deposit in American banks, thinking the money was safer here than in Europe, especially German exporters, who were quite right. More or less for the same reason private European capitalists had been sending money to New York to be employed in short-term paper which they could sell at a moment's notice. And some of Europe's credit balances in this country were simply the untouched proceeds of recent American loans; even the ambulance loans we had made in the summer to avert a financial collapse in Europe. And now what happened to these European credit balances, or rather what they did to us, is what we are about to see.

The Bank of England suspended gold payments for the reason at the very last that as fast as the New York banks could write in their books, "Item, gold credit set aside for the Bank of England on the security of her promissory notes", the European raiders ran to the Bank of England and took the actual gold away, in coin and bullion. The Bank of England in that case was a sieve. When the New York banks stopped writing that item down in their books—"Item, gold credit set aside for the Bank of England"—then immediately the Bank of England stopped paying out her own gold to anybody. She decided, instead, to hoard what she had left, the gold itself in her vaults and also the gold credits on the books of the New York banks.

What followed was a revelation in the abnormal possibilities of international finance. Europe looked westward. The historic habit. For nearly four and a half centuries she has been looking westward for gold. There lay the great American gold reserve, five billions of it, exposed and unprotected. She had keys to it. The keys were those credit balances in New York banks, payable in gold on demand. And where these balances represented, as many of them did, the untouched proceeds of recent American loans to Europe, the keys she had to the American gold reserve were keys we had unwittingly handed away. The American gold reserve was defenseless. There was no way to stop Europe from using those keys, no matter how she had got hold of them. We were foreclosed from making such demands upon Europe as would offset her demands upon us for gold. True, we had enormous bank balances in Europe, but these were either frozen, as in Germany, or now payable in paper money, as in England. In no case could we get gold for them. But Europe could demand all her credit balances in New York to be paid forthwith in gold. True, Europe was owing to the United States Treasury $250,000,000 a year on account of her war debts, and that would have been a large offset against her demands upon us for gold, but we had granted her a one-year moratorium on that obligation, wherefore it was no offset at all. True, we had immense investments in Europe, principally in Germany, but if we sold them we could not get gold for them, whereas German invest- ments in this country could be sold and converted at once into gold. True, we could have sold dollars in Ger- many or dollars in London, but we could not get gold for them, whereas Germany could sell "paper" marks in New York and get gold for them; England could sell paper pounds in New York and get gold for them. The curious and final illustration would be this: that a British holder of a pound sterling note could not go to his own Bank of England and get gold for it, but he could send it to New York, sell it in the foreign exchange market and take the proceeds in gold.

A gold money country must be prepared to honor every kind of paper obligation, not in gold equivalent, not in gold credit, not in something that may be sold somewhere else for gold, but in the gold itself, when, if and as the gold is demanded; and it must do this without demur or hesitation. Therefore, the only protection a gold coun- try has against a run on its gold reserve is to be steadily receiving from its debtors as much as it pays out altogether; its income from foreign countries must equal its outgo to foreign countries, for otherwise it will lose its gold. But we had relieved our debtors. We had eased them of their obligations to us without limiting in any way our obligations to them. One way grace. Thus the abnormity that owing us more than ten billions in the form of public debt on which we had granted a one-year moratorium, in the form of private debt on which we could get nothing in gold even where it was not in default, in the form of overdue short-term credits in Germany and Austria which we had agreed not to demand payment of, in the form of bank balances all over Europe that were simply frozen—owing us all of this, Europe nevertheless could demand payment forthwith and payment in gold of all her credit balances in New York, amounting, as we have supposed, to a billion dollars more or less. And we were obliged either to give up the gold or leave the gold basis ourselves. If we refused the gold in a single case, that instant we were off the gold standard.

How preposterous! Debtors owing us in all manner of ways much more than they can pay, themselves protected by grace, by moratorium or by insolvency, are yet able to descend upon the American gold reserve and deplete it wholesale. During July and August Europe swallows up a billion and a half of American gold credit, much of it without security, simply because she is in despairing need of it; in September she is making a run on the American bank system for gold, and the American bank system is helpless.

We were complacently prepared to lose some gold. We were thinking of Europe and her problems and of ways in which we might help to build England back to the gold standard. One way of helping would be to set no obstacles against a natural movement of gold from this country to Europe. We were willing to sell and lend what gold we could spare. But we were not prepared for a raid.

Not only did Europe demand her deposits with American banks to be paid immediately in gold; she began selling out her short-term American investments, even her American bonds and stocks, and to demand the proceeds in gold, and this at a time when our own internal liquidation was running at flood and the whole American banking structure was under a terrific strain. One of the principal reasons for our own internal liquidation was the frozen and moribund condition of American investments in Europe. For example, American banks were obliged to sell high-class American bonds, even government bonds, because their enormous assets in Europe, especially in Germany, could not be liquidated. Now on top of it all comes this selling of American things by Europe with but one idea, and that is to get the proceeds in gold.

In six weeks we lost $750,000,000 of actual gold coin and bullion. That was nearly one sixth of our entire stock of monetary gold. In less than a year at that rate we should be bare of it.

And it was not simply that Europe's need for this gold was greater than ours, not that the mere possession of it would cure any of her economic ills. The raid was motivated much more by fear and panic than by any economic necessity; nor was that all. Europe wanted the gold for its own sake, wanted it while she could get it—while she had Shylock by the hair. The gold itself! The power of possessing it! The American gold! The temptation to raid us was irresistible.

This strange phase of the situation was presently made clear by the daily figures on where it was going. England did need gold; there was no doubt of that. But to our astonishment, England was not getting it. Of the $750,000,000 we lost out of the American reserve in the first six weeks, France alone took more than one third,—nearly one half—and she did not need it at all, for already she had actually more gold in her possession than any other country, save only the United States, and relatively more than we ourselves possessed.

When the Bank of England suspended gold payments our stock of monetary gold was five billions; the French had two and one third billions. But our population is threefold that of France; our national wealth may be easily five- or sixfold greater. Therefore, France had more gold than this country, in proportion to her economic weight and rank. Our stock of monetary gold was less than $42 per capita; hers was more than $57 per capita. Yet it was France from the beginning that led the run on the American gold reserve.

Why did she want the gold? Was she fearful that the United States would abandon the gold standard? If so, did that fear seize her all at once? That would not be like French bankers. Take their record for it, they see far and straight for France.

In any case, all that France could do with the gold would be to hoard it; and for that purpose she has built since the war a treasure chamber unique in the world. Every country, of course, has massive burglar-proof vaults for its gold reserves. But France decided to make one so deep and strong and mysterious that not even a victorious modern army could break into it. You might blow the Bank of France away with bombs and its gold would be all the safer. The chamber is two and one half acres big; it lies two hundred feet deep in the earth. Over it, first, is forty feet of water, which is a lake they made by damming the subterranean river that flows beneath Paris, and then above the water fifty feet of solid rock. The way to it is through six steel towers with revolving doors moved by electric engines, and the passage of descent can be flooded at a moment's notice. At the signal of alarm a detail of defenders would instantly vanish through this passage, pull the water in after them, and be forgotten—safely forgotten for an indefinite time, or for the duration of a war, because everything has been thought of beforehand. They would find in the gold chamber a kitchen, provisions enough for two or three arctic expeditions, dishes, linen, beds, all the facilities for comfortable housekeeping.

Beginning on or about September 20th, every fast ship from New York for French ports carried gold on its way to this hiding place. The same fast ships or others carried gold also for Holland, Switzerland, Belgium and Germany. Even Germany, where three quarters of a billion of American money was frozen in the form of bank balances and overdue short-term credits—even Germany could take gold from New York.

To lose three quarters of a billion of gold in six weeks, with no saying when or where the run would end and no way of stopping it, was a very serious matter for this country, especially in view of its own condition of internal stress. No country, under any conditions, could lose gold at that rate or in that proportion for long and hold to the gold standard. That would be true if to begin with it had all the gold in the world.

We had only ourselves to blame. One-way grace; no means of self-protection reserved. We were caught by our gold heel in a trap we had built for ourselves. We made it and walked straight in. It was not inevitable that we should have exposed our gold reserve, without protection, to an unlimited foreign attack. Once we had done it, however, the attack, all the natural consequences, were inevitable. But this is not to say the total of Europe's behavior was only such as we might have expected. By instance, who could have foreseen that parallel to the raid on the American gold reserve there would run in Europe a campaign of rumor, innuendo and propaganda against the value of the American dollars? That also happened, and it certainly was not inevitable, not even from our naïve point of view.

In France the campaign was subtle and ingenious; in England frank and brutal. As the Bank of France took gold from New York, rumors of an imminent financial collapse in the United States spread from Paris throughout Europe and the French papers kept saying with one voice that the franc was the sound gold money of the world. Then came the news that President Hoover had called upon American bankers to mobilize the credit resources of the American banking system against the tide of liquidation that was running in New York—much of it foreign liquidation in order to produce gold for Europe—and instantly, upon the raw news, without waiting for details, the leaders of current opinion in France pronounced a sensational judgment. The United States, they said, had entered the path to inflation. This was the beginning of the end of the gold dollar. Would the people now believe it? The franc was the good gold money of the world.

Immediately in all the financial capitals of Europe the value of the American dollar declined. In Poland, where the dollar had been for years a standard unit of value, serving even as security for the Polish currency, there was a dollar panic. The *New York Times* correspondent at Warsaw cabled, October 9: "A flight from the dollar started here this morning on the heels of alarming reports from Paris that the United States Government had decided to abandon the gold standard and that an increase in the issue of dollar notes was being discussed in Washington." In one day the Polish people, remembering what inflation was like, sold one million American dollars to the Bank of Warsaw at ninety-nine cents. The panic lasted several days and then subsided in a bewildered realization that the Paris rumors were false.

The British campaign was led by the Rothemere newspapers, which have a combined daily circulation of five millions. Day after day these papers printed under big headlines the editorial opinion that the downfall of American credit was at hand, together with the exhortation to sell dollars and dollar securities while yet there was time to convert them into gold. Examples: "BRING YOUR MONEY BACK TO BRITAIN.—Advices from America indicate a serious state of affairs. This, therefore offers a favorable moment to sell dollar securities and bring back the money to this country." Again: "SELL DOLLAR AND FRANC SECURITIES.—Don't be trapped. When the break on Wall Street comes, the reaction may be far-reaching." Another day: "WHO WILL GO OFF THE GOLD STANDARD NEXT?—The American banking position shows no sign of improvement." And so on, in such taste and meaning, day after day, with the Bank of England and the British Treasury together owing New York 350,000,000 gold dollars.

The financial nerves of the world are taut. They have been plucked and frayed to the snapping point. All the shapes of insolvency are dim. At this moment the premier of France must pay a visit to the President of the United States to examine with him the problems of the world and explore all solutions.

What is it France wants? We already know in principle, even in some particulars, what she wants. First, she wants to get rid of her war debts to the United States Treasury. She wishes the American Government to forgive her these debts and charge them to the American taxpayer. Until this can happen she wants to continue receiving reparations from Germany. Therefore, she wants to save the Young Plan, which Germany, England and many Americans, too, have taken for dead since the London conference last summer, especially since the report of the Wiggins Committee of Experts. The reason why she wants to save the Young Plan is that it stipulates for certain large unconditional annuities to be paid by Germany to France before any one else shall receive reparations at all. She does not want the Hoover war debt holiday to be extended beyond its year; she prefers to be receiving more money from Germany on account of reparations than she pays to the United States Treasury on account of her war debts, as it was before. The holiday came very near to costing her $100,000,000 a year, which was the excess of her German reparations over her payments to the United States Treasury; and it would have cost her that if she had not demanded special treatment as a preferred German creditor. Then in principle France wants anything else that will increase her power and prestige in the world.

What has any of this to do with the gold crisis? Well, what it all has to do with the gold crisis now immediately appears.

With the premier of France on the high seas in this direction, and with the newspapers running big headlines on the momentous nature of his visit, suddenly we are astonished by the news that the Bank of France has served an ultimatum on the American banking system. The ultimatum is this: France cannot afford to leave her credit balances in New York any longer unless the rate of interest is raised. If the rate of interest is not raised she will feel obliged to call the remainder of her credit balances home. And the remainder of these credit balances is $600,000,000.

This is as the news appeared in the *New York Times* on the morning of October 20: "The Bank of France, which has about $600,000,000 of short-term balances in this market, yesterday notified New York banks that the $1\frac{1}{2}$ per cent. rate of interest now being paid on foreign central bank deposits by local institutions was unsatisfactory. The French bank of issue indicated that unless a higher rate was provided it would seek other employment for its huge dollar balances.

"The French demand for a higher rate of interest, carrying with it the implied threat of withdrawal of French dollar balances in the form of gold, aroused a mixed reaction in Wall Street. Some bankers, who interpreted the move as an attempt to dictate to this market the terms under which France would refrain from re-

calling her money, flatly declared that they were willing
to see the funds go. They said, despite the heavy gold
losses recently sustained by the country, the United States
had nothing to fear from such action on the part of
France and much to gain by getting rid of an unwieldy
obligation that, under other circumstances, might prove
embarrassing. Other important bankers expressed the
belief that the Bank of France would be satisfied with
a slightly higher rate, possibly two per cent., and were
inclined to stress this viewpoint as an indication that
amicable arrangements for maintaining French balances
here intact could be reached."

Firstly, the figure was astounding. For a long time
France had been doing here what she did in England,
namely, accumulate enormous credit balances. The
amount of them was much more than we realized, much
more than Wall Street itself knew, since of course they
were not all in one place.

Secondly, what did these French credit balances represent? Besides the normal proceeds of trade left on
deposit with American banks, they represented (a) dollar
checks cashed by American tourists in France, and (b)
American money loaned to Germany to pay reparations
to France. These transactions are easily understood. As
the French banks cashed the dollar checks of American
tourists they took credit for them in American banks.
This credit in American banks was gold credit; therefore
the Bank of France treated it as gold reserve, as if it were
gold actually in hand, and issued French currency against
it for circulation in France. And the same way with
American credit loaned to Germany to pay reparations.
The Germans transferred it to France on the books of
American banks and the French left it here at interest.

Thirdly, how oblique that France, our debtor, owing
us in one pocket 3¾ billions of dollars on which she is
paying us this year nothing, may yet demand 600 millions of gold from another pocket! She has that right.

If she insists, we shall have to give her the gold. But she can do this only because her payments to the United States Treasury are suspended for a year by grace of an American moratorium.

Fourthly, such a thing as the central bank of one country serving notice on the banking system of another country that because the rate of interest is too low, or for any reason, it may feel obliged to call its aggregate credit balances away in gold, was hitherto unheard of. No one could have imagined it. That is not the way it happens in the normal course of international finance. Credit balances are continually shifting. If the rate of interest is higher in New York than in London, credit balances move automatically to New York, or if the rate of interest is higher in London they shift from New York to London, and nothing is ever said about it. The only news of it will be in the bank statistics.

Now, the Bank of France very well knew that suddenly to lose $600,000,000 more gold, on top of what we had already lost to Europe—and the bulk of it to France—would create a very grave situation in this country. And mark this, that if the French themselves believed what they had been saying in Europe about the dollar and about the American financial situation in general they must have believed that to demand $600,000,000 more gold all at once from New York would pitch this country off the gold standard. Well, of course, in that event—in the event of the dollar going the way of the pound sterling —then the French franc assuredly would be the premier gold money and govern the world of finance.

Did she mean it? That is a very interesting question. As a proposition in pure finance you would suppose that if the Bank of France had really meant to call away her $600,000,000 credit balance in gold she would not have been so stupid as to announce her whole intention beforehand. Any village banker would know better. Actually, therefore, the Bank of France was probably bluffing.

The Bank of France is to France what the Bank of England is to Great Britain. In finance it is France. Therefore it would have been France that was bluffing and this carries it at once beyond finance into high politics.

Under pretence of being dissatisfied with the rate of interest in New York the Bank of France revealed to us, to Europe, to the whole world, the amazing fact that France had the power, almost if not quite, to throw the American banking system off the gold standard! To send the American dollar after the pound sterling!

That was something for the premier of France to have in his hand when he should begin to examine the problems of the world and explore solutions with Mr. Hoover in the White House. But it was at the same time a revelation in no way calculated to relieve the tension then existing here and elsewhere or to check the hoarding of gold by individuals—a dread movement that was already world-wide and threatening to become uncontrollable.

There were some very anxious moments in Washington. Public utterances were guarded and censored and hushed, lest something should get said out loud to offend the feelings of France. What would Wall Street do? What could it do? If it were willing to raise the rate of interest, on the ultimatum of the Bank of France, still, to do so would be to acknowledge the power of France. But if it refused, then what would happen? Would France really demand the gold?

But there was only one right thing for Wall Street to say. May it be long remembered to the credit of Wall Street that it did say it. To this effect: "We pay here the New York rate of interest, whatever that may be. If France wants her credit balances, let her take them. If she demands them in gold, the gold will be ready."

The right honorable *Financial Chronicle*, with its Biblical prestige in Wall Street, said: "The move was resented as an attempt to bring financial pressure to bear on the United States after the fashion that has been followed from time to time in recent European political manœuvers.

"Bankers here are confident that the country has nothing to fear from such a move, provided the American people themselves remain undisturbed. We think this is a proper attitude for our banking institutions to take. France contributed in no unimportant degree to the financial breakdown in Germany by withdrawing large amounts of short-term credits which it had employed in that country, its action then being followed by general withdrawal of credits and deposits by other foreign governments. It was then supposed that its purpose was mainly political. But later it began also to indulge in withdrawals of capital and of funds from Great Britain, though when the French bank became alarmed as to the possible consequences it once more began to coöperate to extend new credits to the Bank of England and to Great Britain. But it was now too late to save Great Britain from suspension of gold payments.

"In like manner France is now engaged in huge withdrawals from New York, though we cannot get ourselves to believe that the Bank of France has any ulterior purpose in doing this. At all events, the effect has been to create a feeling of distrust all over Europe and to lead to large withdrawals here by other important European countries, and more particularly Holland, Belgium and Switzerland. In these circumstances the best course is unquestionably to ignore all threats (if such have really been made) and to let France do her worst if she is really bent on doing so."

Any other way of speaking to the Bank of France would have stultified American credit in the eyes of the world. The effect of that way of speaking was immediate. In all foreign financial capitals the dollar rose to new prestige and its value increased. When the disordered events of 1929 come to be viewed in perspective, it may well appear that Wall Street's strong-minded behavior at this point was of crucial importance, not only to this country but to a world that needed more than anything else just then a point of stability whereon to rest its confidence.

So it turned out that when the premier of France landed in New York what he had in his hand was not the bolt it was when he started with it. Nevertheless, he could not help using it for magnanimous effect. He pledged France to assist the United States in maintaining the gold standard.

In the joint statement issued from the White House on October 25 by President Hoover and Premier Laval this paragraph occurred: "Particularly are we convinced of the importance of monetary stability as an essential factor in the restoration of the normal economic life in the world, in which the maintenance of the gold standard in France and the United States will serve as a major influence."

And what would be the French contribution to the monetary stability of the world? What would France do to assist the United States in maintaining the gold standard? This, to wit: Pending a reëxamination of her war debt to the United States Treasury, pending further a reexamination of Germany's capacity to pay under the Young Plan which makes France the preferred creditor, France would make no more abnormal demands upon the American gold reserve.

In his news report of the Hoover-Laval conversations the Washington correspondent of the *New York Times,* October 26, wrote: "In a cautious way the joint statement made known that President Hoover and Premier Laval had determined that their two governments should stand together in their maintenance of the gold standard. Among the things accomplished were the reassurance by Premier Laval that abnormal movements of gold from New York would be stopped, and that reëxamination of Germany's capacity to pay reparations should be made

under the existing provisions of the Young Plan, with the
United States deferring action on a survey of European
debts to determine the capacity of debtor nations to pay
until after a Young Plan committee has reported on
Germany's financial position."

Abnormal is a strange word to be appearing in respect to the demands of one nation upon the gold reserves of another. In respect to the demands of a debtor
nation upon the gold reserves of its creditor it grows
stranger. And that the debtor nation should be able to
oblige the creditor nation by a pledge to restrain itself
from making abnormal demands upon the creditor's gold
reserve is more than strange. Why any possibility of
abnormal demands by France upon the American gold
reserve?

Then again, what is abnormal? Did M. Laval mean
abnormal in principle, perhaps? He sailed away on Monday, October 26. On that day the Bank of France took
$20,000,000 more gold from New York, on Tuesday
$18,000,000, but on Wednesday only $3,500,000. Yet
$41,500,000 gold in three days is certainly a great deal.
However, there were signs by then that the tide was beginning to turn. Still losing gold heavily to France we
were again receiving gold at the same time because the
dollar at last was thinking to mind its own welfare and
the world's confidence in American credit was rising.

A gold country is like a bank. Its first responsibility
is to itself, for the integrity of its money, its credit and
its assets, and if it suffers this imperative to be overcome
by a sense of responsibility to others, no matter with what
intention, it will fail in its responsibility to others because
it has forgotten that first responsibility to itself. There is
no other law.

In one of the bad moments last October a member of
the Federal Reserve Board was heard to say: "Not only
is this the worst financial crisis in all history. Something
is missing that was always there before. All over the

world there is this sense of something missing, like a familiar rock, an immovable principle, a wheel of balance. And what is it? The Bank of England is missing. The value of the pound sterling is uncertain, changing from hour to hour. We never had that to contend with before."

So it was. And that is why the suspension of gold payments by the Bank of England was an appalling financial event. No longer was the pound sterling worth $4.86 in gold anywhere in the world. No longer was it the universal unit of value in which all other things were priced. Now the pound sterling itself has to be priced in other things—in American dollars, for example. Then suppose the same thing should happen to the dollar, which had recently become the next most stable unit of value in the world's opinion. Suppose the dollar, instead of being worth one hundred cents in gold anywhere in the world, should have to be priced at ninety cents, eighty cents, seventy cents, in terms of something else, maybe the French franc.

The long and familiar preëminence of the pound sterling as a universal unit of value in any kind of financial weather, war only excepted, had been worth to Great Britain an income of three or four hundred millions a year from the rest of the world in the form of banking profit, meaning discounts, commissions, interest and fees. Preëminence of the American dollar in the trade and exchange of the world, in place of the pound sterling, would be worth 300 or 400 millions a year to this country. Or, if such preëminence passed to the French franc, it would be worth 300 or 400 millions a year to France.

So you may see what was involved as between the dollar and the franc, merely in terms of national income; you may see also what Great Britain had lost. You may understand at the same time that when the British say it was a good thing for England to leave the gold standard they mean only that it was good for England that she embraced a bitter necessity in time, for if she had waited, her

fortunes might have become irretrievable. Now she will
work harder, trade harder, spend less, live a little less,
until she is quite solvent again. Her export of goods will
increase for several reasons. They will be priced in the
depreciated pound sterling, which means they will be
cheaper for the world to buy, or, to say it another way,
other people's gold money will buy more in England
than before. Prices will rise in England, but not as much
as the value of the pound sterling declines outside; as
prices rise in England, real wages will fall, wherefore
the labor cost of producing British goods will fall, and so
will the standard of living in England, temporarily at
least. And this must all happen to any country that loses
the integrity of its money.

True, you will hear some British economists say it
was not England that failed the gold standard; it was
the gold standard that failed the world. Therefore, they
say, the world may do well to try something in place of
the gold standard and see if that will work any better.
This is a novel way of thinking in England, yet elsewhere very old—putting the blame on money! If England had not lost her hold on the gold standard she would
be the last to say the gold standard had not been working
—in a remorseless manner, to be sure, yet nevertheless
working as it should—in the last three years. If she had
not lost her hold on it and other countries were losing
theirs, the Bank of England would be saying: "This is
hard, but it is the way the gold standard works." It
would be a grim thing to say, a selfish thing, perhaps,
and yet quite right. For how did the pound sterling
come to have preëminence throughout the world in the
first place? Its prestige was from the fact that the British
had always a primary sense of their responsibility to
themselves, that is to say, again, for the integrity of their
own money and their own credit; and it turned out, as
the law is, that the more jealous they were in this first
sense of responsibility to themselves the more certain they

were not to fail the world in their responsibilities to it, including the responsibility to keep the balance wheel running true. Thus the pound sterling became a symbol of stability that was a great asset to the whole world.

THE GOLD INVENTION

Always, man pursueth himself with a broken law.

The true meaning of the gold standard is not gold, any more than the value of a piece of paper money is in the quality of the engraving. The true meaning of it is a convention and the faith of that convention must be kept, not in gold, but in credit. Gold is the accidental figure in which the convention is embodied. It might be almost anything else, except that after long experience it was found that gold served better than anything else, merely as the figure. Once it was silver. The pound sterling originally was a pound of silver. The American dollar was originally silver. Yet when the figure was silver the convention was the same; so also were the penalties for breaking the faith.

The value of gold is arbitrary; so is the length of a yardstick. But just as it is necessary to sell cloth by the yard or coal by the ton, so it is necessary to have some arbitrary unit of value in which to price the yard of cloth and the ton of coal. It would be ideal to have something of absolutely invariable value in which to price them. But there is no absolutely invariable thing in the world. The relative constancy of the gold supply, the durability of the metal, the fact that over the centuries the amount of human exertion necessary to get it out of the rocks changes very slowly—for these and other reasons gold is the least unstable thing man has found for purposes of money, hence his preference for it.

Once the quantity of it was important, merely as money.

That is no longer true. The total stock of monetary gold in the world could be stored in one small barn. Yet if the mechanism of credit and exchange were perfect and all people could be trusted, by themselves and by one another, to keep the convention, one ton of it, one ounce of it, in fact, would serve the modern purpose.

One of the singular characteristics of gold is its extensibility. Between two pieces of fine leather made from the intestines of an ox it may be beaten to the impalpable thickness of 1/300,000th part of an inch, so that one troy grain may be made to cover 56 square inches. On the number of pure gold leaves, 4″ x 7″, that could be beaten from one ounce, worth $20.60, you could print the Old Testament in the ordinary Bible type, if the leaves would bear printing.

The ancient goldbeater's art may astonish the senses. More astonishing to the imagination is the extensibility of gold in a fictional dimension. Out of this same tame and friendly metal, men have beaten a pure fiction of gold, the very spirit of it, and this fiction or spirit is infinitely extensible and infinitely divisible. The gross name for this fiction or spirit of gold is credit. The business of extending and dividing the spirit—the business, that is to say, of creating credit and setting it free— is in the hands of bankers, banking systems and governments; and the convention, namely, the true meaning of the gold standard, is simply their undertaking that the amount of credit created and set free shall bear a certain relation, called a ratio, to the amount of actual gold in their possession. The ratio is variable, from time to time. If and as the business of the world increases faster than the gold supply, so that there is really a need for more money and credit, the ratio may be raised.

It is not the ratio itself that is so all-important, as many people think, especially debtors who are always wanting cheap money with which to pay their debts, or, on the other hand, creditors, whose advantage is in dear money. The imperatives are simple and three.

First, that there shall be some definite ratio.

Second, that it shall have been agreed upon when we were all in our right minds.

Third, that we hold to it in good faith.

For this now is the modern function of gold—to limit the amount of money and credit that may be wilfully, irresponsibly created and set free.

Organized credit is relatively a strange thing in the economic life. New and experimental forms of it are continually being invented and we love to deceive ourselves with them. We forget that credit in any form represents debt in some other form. We know about ourselves that we have seizures of ecstasy and mass delusion; that again a time may come when the temptation to throw the monetary machine into wild motion so that everybody may become infinitely rich by means of infinite debt will rise to the pitch of mania, as it did, for example, in 1928 and 1929. With this intelligent knowledge of ourselves we make bargains beforehand with reason; we agree that money, credit and debt shall not be inflated beyond a certain ratio to gold, under certain penalties such as we shall be very loath to pay and yet such as we cannot refuse to pay under worse penalties still.

So long as the convention is reasonably kept in the faith of credit nobody wants gold. People know what the fiction is. They may read for themselves in the published figures of the bank that its liabilities exceed its gold tenor twentyfold, and yet they feel no anxiety about the gold value of their deposits. They may read for themselves in the figures from the public treasury that the gold reserve is only one half or one third as much as the amount of paper money in circulation. Yet they will treat that paper money as if it were gold. Nobody would dream of supposing that a country, no matter how rich, could redeem its bonds in gold. Yet its bonds will be treated as if they were gold, and one who happens to want gold for them may freely have it. All so long as the convention is kept.

Does this mean, as some of the silly textbooks used to say, that we are all gambling upon a mythical law of averages? No. It means a very definite thing. It means that if every kind of physical wealth were priced in gold, all in one moment of inventory, the aggregate value of it would not be less than the total amount of money, credit and debt outstanding against it. Then all the money is as good as gold, all the credit is gold credit, gold itself is a nuisance in the pocket.

But let the faith be broken, let the delusion arise that the fiction is the reality, let the limit upon the amount of credit that shall be set free be left to imagination, and presently there is no way of telling what anything is worth by pricing it.

For a while this difficulty of not knowing what anything is worth but inflames the ecstasy. Everything will be priced higher and higher to make sure it is high enough; there will be the illusion that things are becoming dear and scarce. They seem to be dear because the value of the money and credit in which they are priced is falling; they will seem to be scarce because people are buying in the expectation that prices will go higher and higher still. Suddenly doubt, then coming awake and panic. The spirit of gold has been debased by senseless inflation. The faith is lost. All with one impulse people rush to seize the gold itself as the only reality left—not only people as individuals; banks, also, and the great banking systems and governments do it, in competition with people. This is the financial crisis.

All of it has happened. It was not the gold standard that did it; it was breaking faith with the gold standard that did it, and the case would be the same if the standard were anything else.

And who is responsible for breaking the faith? In this country no one is responsible. American banking is governed by law; the law assumes that bankers cannot be trusted not to ruin themselves and their depositors. Therefore, we have more laws to mind banking practice than any other people—and more bank failures in spite of them. The federal and state governments employ thousands of examiners who go round and round, looking into the private books of the banks to see if they are solvent and law-keeping, and the law says that when they find one to be insolvent they must shut it up immediately. And still they fail.

We go on the assumption that a bank is more interested in gain than in its own solvency and if it is not watched its greed for gain will wreck it. Therefore it must be policed. Examiners clothed with arbitrary power must appear at unexpected moments, taking the bank by surprise in any wickedness, and say: "Throw open your books." And yet they fail.

It will be always impossible to keep a bank solvent by law. The law that specifies the maximum risk a bank may legally take with other people's money turns out to be a law of minimum security. A good banker will not take a risk simply because the law says he may; he will use his own judgment. On the other hand, a reckless banker will find a way to do what his greed desires, no matter what the law is, even a legal way.

BOOK OF THE DEBTS

I

"To wipe out all that."
—RAMSAY MACDONALD
PRIME MINISTER OF ENGLAND

On war debts and reparations,
in his election speeches, 1931.

"This crude job jocularly called a settlement."
—LLOYD GEORGE,

Referring to the British agree-
ment with the United States
Treasury, in his book entitled,
"The Truth About War Debts
And Reparations", 1932.

In the spring of 1917 the star of Germanity was over-
coming. "It cannot be said," wrote General Pershing in
his Final Report, "that German hopes of a final victory
were extravagant, either as viewed at that time or as
viewed in the light of history. Financial problems of the
Allies were difficult, supplies were becoming exhausted,
and their armies had suffered tremendous losses. Dis-
couragement existed not only among the civil populations
but throughout the armies as well."

The financial case was desperate. The Allies were
staring at the end of their credit.

In March, before the United States had embraced the
war, the American Ambassador to Great Britain sent a

letter home to his brother, saying: "My staff and I are asking everybody what the Americans can best do to help the cause along. The views are not startling but they are interesting. Jellicoe: More ships, merchant ships, any kind of ships. Balfour: Credits in the United States big enough to keep up the rate of exchange. Bonar Law: Same thing. The military men: An expeditionary force, no matter how small, for the effect of the American flag in Europe."

What Balfour meant by credits enough to keep up the rate of exchange was anything to support the exchange value of the British pound sterling, or, that is to say, its buying power in other countries, most importantly its buying power in the markets of the United States. Credit —American credit—meant more food, more supplies, more munitions, even the ships Jellicoe wanted. Credit meant everything but man power; and the problem of man power was yet less acute than the problem of credit. A small expeditionary force, if only a regiment, to take the American flag to the front for its effect on their morale—yes, that was very desirable. But first of all, credit.

"By their own admission, at the time we came into the situation, the Allies were at their wits' end to know which way to turn in order to obtain needed supplies. When the United States opened her pocketbook all was changed. The outcome we know. Our help ended the war. We supplied in almost unlimited volume the munitions required to enable the Allies to go on fighting while we were enrolling and training men. When the armistice was signed we had all but two million men in France. Within six months we would have had twice that number there. To conserve shipping to get these men across, we bought great quantities of munitions in Europe. We paid higher prices for these goods than we would have needed to pay at home, even with the cost of ocean transportation added, but it was better to do this and save shipping for the men." From "The Inter-Ally Debts," by Harvey E. Fisk, published by the Bankers Trust Company of New York, 1924.

On April 6, 1917, the United States entered the war, as an associate, not as an ally. This distinction was jealously maintained to the end of the war, through the armistice period and at the Peace Conference.

Four days later the chairman of the Ways and Means Committee introduced in Congress the first Liberty Bond Act with these words: "This bill contains the largest authorization of bond issues ever contained in any bill presented to any legislative body in the history of the world."

It authorized the Secretary of the Treasury to borrow five billions of dollars on the credit of the American Government; and of this incredible sum of five billions to be raised at once by the sale of Liberty Bonds three fifths was for the purpose of buying at par the bonds of foreign governments at war with Germany. That was the credit the Allies were in desperate need of; and that was the beginning of the war debts. Within two weeks the bill was passed.

The first advance could not wait on the preparation and sale of Liberty Bonds. The United States Treasury borrowed money on its own notes to make the initial loan to Great Britain.

What this meant to Great Britain was described by the notable pen of Ambassador Page in a letter to President Wilson, dated London, May 4: "I heard all the speeches in both houses on the resolution of appreciation of our coming into the war. It wasn't oratory but it was well said and well meant. They know how badly they need help and they do mean to be as good to us as their benignant insularity will permit. They are changing. I can't describe the great difference that the war has made to them. They'll almost become docile in a little more time. And we came in the nick of time for them—very true. If we hadn't, their exchange would have gone down soon and they know it. I shall never forget the afternoon I spent with Mr. Balfour and Mr. Bonar Law on that subject. They saw blue ruin without our financial help."

By subsequent acts, as the credit was required, Congress voted seven billions of dollars more from the proceeds of Liberty Bonds to be loaned to foreign governments on their unsecured promissory notes, which were received temporarily in lieu of bonds; always these notes were to be replaced later by bonds running parallel to the Liberty Bonds on which the American Government borrowed the money. The total amount so authorized was ten billions. All subsequent acts, however, were merely extensional. It was understood that our undertaking to provide credit was unlimited and the character of the transactions had been definitely established.

American Treasury loans to foreign governments, beginning in April, 1917, ended in November, 1920, and amounted, net, to somewhat less than eleven billions of dollars. They fall under three main headings, namely:

(a) pre-armistice loans,

(b) post-armistice loans, and

(c) loans after the war for relief, for reconstruction, for mopping up, and to enable European governments to buy a great quantity of surplus American property in Europe. This last named item in France alone was 400 millions.

Direct cash advances from the United States Treasury to foreign governments, pre-armistice, were a little more than 7 billions. Direct cash advances from the United States Treasury to foreign governments, post-armistice, were a little more than 2⅓ billions.

And all of this represented money raised by the American Government both from the sale of Liberty Bonds and by taxation and reloaned to foreign governments. By far the greater part of it was from the proceeds of Liberty Bonds, and those Liberty Bonds are still outstanding in the hands of the American people. Congress never imagined redeeming them out of American taxes. It was taken for granted that the foreign governments were going to redeem the obligations they delivered to the United States Treasury as they got the money; and as they redeemed their obligations the United States Treasury automatically would redeem the parallel Liberty Bonds.

"The indebtedness incurred by the United States to make the foreign loans is not cared for by the sinking fund. Congress contemplated that foreign repayments would provide for that part of our debt."—Report of the Secretary of the Treasury, 1920, page 64.

II

"A loan should come laughing home."
—OLD PROVERB

As to the character of these American Treasury loans to foreign governments, a controversy that was invented in Europe immediately after the war has continued ever since, with increasing ill-will, confusion of fact and emotional bitterness. Were they by nature formal transactions between nations, subject to the terms and sequels of financial usage, or had they a meaning such as to make interest, accounting, settlement and repayment repugnant? Not now—not since they have come to be invested with feeling from ceaseless dispute and propaganda—but in the beginning how were they understood?

The answer, if it exists, would be found—

(a) in the law itself,

(b) in the contract,

(c) in the attitude of the borrowers at the time, if there is any record of that, and

(d) in the use the borrowers made of the money; that is to say, in facts tending to show whether their use of it was as that of borrowers who mean to pay it back with interest and have therefore full and unlimited rights in it, or otherwise.

The law was explicit.

Section 2 of the First Liberty Loan Act reads as follows:

"That for the purpose of more effectually providing for the national security and defense and prosecuting the war, by establishing credits by the United States for foreign governments, the Secretary of the Treasury, with the approval of the President, is hereby authorized, on behalf of the United States, to purchase, at par, from such foreign governments then engaged in war with the enemies of the United States, their obligations hereafter issued, bearing the same rate of interest and containing in their essentials the same terms and conditions as those of the United States issued under the authority of this Act."

In bringing this bill before Congress, the Ways and Means Committee of the House made the following unanimous statement:

"It authorizes the purchase with the proceeds from the sale of these (Liberty) bonds of the obligations of foreign governments bearing the same rate of interest and containing essentially the same terms and conditions as the (Liberty) bonds issued under authority of this act. It provides that should any of the (Liberty) bonds of the United States issued and used for the purchase of such foreign obligations be converted into United States bonds bearing a higher rate of interest . . . that in such events the obligations of the foreign governments held by the United States shall be converted into obligations bearing the same rate of interest as the like bonds of the United States. It will, therefore, be observed that the $3,-000,000,000 credit proposed to be extended to foreign governments will take care of itself and will not constitute an indebtedness that will have to be met by taxation in the future."

In the course of debate several objections were raised. One was that we were proposing to buy the obligations of foreign governments at par, whereas their bonds were already selling at a discount. To this the chairman of the Ways and Means Committee replied: "If their bonds have gone down to 80 or 75 or 50 per cent., all the more necessity exists for us to loan them this money at the lowest possible rate of interest, because they are helping to fight our cause."

Another objection was that the law did not restrain the borrowers in their use of the money; for example, it did not require them to spend the money in this country, nor was there anything in it to prevent them from using money out of the American Treasury to pay off other loans in Wall Street. To this the chairman of the Ways and Means Committee answered: "Why not leave it to them to expend the proceeds in any way which their judgment tells them is the best way to achieve success?" By necessity most of the money would be spent in this country, he said, and as for their using it to pay off other loans maturing in Wall Street, he could hardly conceive of it, and yet: "Why limit or qualify the use of the money?"

There were many emotional passages. That would be expected. Those who showed too much anxiety about the safety of the loans were rebuked by others who said security was not what we ought to be thinking of. Some kept saying the borrowers were fighting our battles. This provoked a gentleman from Pennsylvania to say: "I do not like the suggestion that the reason we propose to lend them the proceeds of our bonds is to reward them for 'fighting our battles.' My view is that these foreign governments are fighting their own battles and that we are aiding them. When we lend these foreign countries money we are rendering them an assistance and they are not rendering assistance to us." A gentleman from Virginia said he wished it were possible to write into the bill a "forbearance and remittance upon any French bonds purchased by the American Government," and this sentiment was applauded.

In the Senate the debate was of the same pattern.

The facts are that Congress entertained no proposal to treat the loans as gifts or subsidies, nor otherwise at all than as loans, strictly repayable with interest, and that the bill as quoted became a law by unanimous vote in both House and Senate.

All the contracts were formal. There was, however, some deviation from the law. It provided that we were to buy the bonds of foreign governments, their bonds to be parallel in terms and interest to the Liberty Bonds sold by the American Government to raise the money; but there was never time to prepare the bonds, and for that reason the United States Treasury accepted from foreign governments, in lieu of bonds, their promissory notes. This was the note:

"The government of [name of foreign country], for value received, promises to pay to the United States of America, or assigns, the sum of [number of dollars in words] on demand, with interest from the date hereof at the rate of [blank] per cent. per annum. . . . This certificate will be converted by the government of [name of foreign country] if requested by the Secretary of the Treasury of the United States of America, at par, with an adjustment of accrued interest, into an equal amount of [rate] per cent. convertible gold bonds of the government of [name of foreign country], conforming to the provisions of acts of Congress of the United States.

(Signed "By its representative.

"For the government [name of foreign country]"
"Dated the . . . . . . day of . . . ."

When the direct cash advances ceased, in November, 1920, the American Treasury held such notes to the face value of nearly ten billions. They were separately signed by eleven foreign governments. The principals were—

Great Britain	for	$4,277,000,000
France	for	2,997,477,000
Italy	for	1,631,338,987
Belgium	for	349,214,468
Russia	for	187,729,750

As to the attitude of the borrowers, it is to be said first that never during the war was there any suggestion coming from them that the terms were hard or ungenerous, or that the loans were not loans in a strict financial sense, repayable in full with interest. France explicitly rejected the idea of special treatment, or that she should receive anything as a gift or subsidy.

On April 11, 1917, while the first Liberty Loan Act was pending in Congress, and the gentleman from Virginia saying he wished it were possible to write into the law some "forbearance and remittance" in the case of France, the American Ambassador to France wired from Paris to the Secretary of State in Washington as follows:

"The Premier personally expressed the hope to me that no resolution would be introduced or debated in Congress tending to make a gift to the government of France from the United States, however much the sentiment of good will prompting it might be appreciated by the French people."

There is more to the same point in this part of the record. *Le Matin* of Paris published portions of a cable exchange between the French Premier and the French Ambassador to the United States as follows:

"DIPLOMATIE PARIS   April 12, 1917.

"I have just had an interview with the Secretary of the Treasury regarding our financial needs. The amount of $133,000,000 a month drew no observation from him; the amount of $218,000,000 which would be reached by adding our expenses outside the United States, appeared high to him, but it is not impossible that we shall get it. . . .

As to the term for repayment, I mentioned (supposing this to be desirable) that of 15 years. Mr. McAdoo said that he had no objection to that.

(Signed) JUSSERAND."

"April 17, 1917.
"I shall do my best in the matter of repayment in 25 years. . . . I believed that I had good reason to suppose that 15 years would be considered satisfactory.

(Signed) JUSSERAND."

"Paris, April 19, 1917.
"French Ambassador, Washington.
The Minister of Finance insists that the term of amortization shall be 30 years, a normal and minimum term in such operations.

(Signed) RIBOT."

In the settlements that have been so much disputed about France did receive special treatment. The amount to be repaid was reduced practically to post-armistice loans, and the term of repayment was made, not thirty years, as the French themselves had suggested as the normal minimum in such operations, but sixty-two years. That in its place.

Immediately upon the intervention of the United States as a belligerent, on the side of the Allies, England and France sent missions to this country to discuss coöperation. Head of the British mission was Arthur J. Balfour, Foreign Minister and former premier of Great Britain. His part was diplomacy. With him came Lord Cunliffe, governor of the Bank of England; his part was finance. Head of the French mission was M. Viviani, Minister of Justice; his associate and financial adviser was M. Simon, Inspector of Finance. The first business of these missions was finance.

As part of its campaign to sell Liberty Bonds the

United States Treasury, in 1917, issued a long, popular statement telling why we were lending the proceeds of Liberty Bonds to foreign government and the meaning of such loans. The money was not a contribution to the Allies, our associates; it was loaned to them and would ultimately be repaid in full. That view was very positive; also the view that the Allies were perfectly solvent; the only trouble was that they were in need of ready money. And if it should seem that one effect of these loans was to uphold their own trade and commerce, so much the better. It was sound economic policy on our part to assist them to uphold their industrial life and commercial welfare. That made them all the stronger, as belligerents and as creditors.

In these views and representations the foreign missions heartily collaborated. They were undoubtedly sincere; everybody was. It is the record.

"The foreign governments were required by the Treasury to state the purposes to be served in order to enable the Treasury to determine whether they were germane to the purposes indicated by the Liberty Loan Acts and whether and in what amounts credits should be given. The Treasury did not, of course, make expenditures for the foreign governments. It paid to them the purchase price of the securities; and they made the expenditures."—Report of the Secretary of the Treasury, 1920, p. 69.

But in the view of the American Treasury at the time almost anything tending to promote the morale and welfare of the Allies, even the welfare of their industry and commerce, was considered germane. And this leads to the matter of how the money actually was spent—as if the borrowers had full rights in it because they meant to pay it back with interest, or otherwise.

On page 340 of the annual report of the Secretary of the Treasury, year 1920, exhibit 27, appears the following summary of what they did with the money:

Expenditures:
For—

Munitions for themselves	$ 2,493,610,325
Munitions for other governments	205,495,810
Exchange and cotton purchases	2,644,783,870
Cereals	1,422,476,706
Other foods	1,629,726,803
Tobacco	145,100,821
Other supplies	613,107,429
Transportation	136,083,775
Shipping	173,397,084
Reimbursements	1,872,914,604
Interest	730,504,177
Maturities	648,246,317
Relief	538,188,330
Silver	267,943,389
Food for Northern Russia	7,029,966
Purchases from neutrals	18,718,579
Special credit for Italy against American expenditures in Italy	25,000,000
Miscellaneous	168,530,576
Total reported expenditures	$13,740,858,551

Deduct:
For—

Reimbursements from United States credits to other governments	$ 1,872,914,604
Dollar payments by United States government for foreign currencies	1,490,557,908
Proceeds of rupee credits and gold from India	81,352,908
Total deductions	$ 3,444,824,623

Net expenditures reported by foreign governments

$10,296,033,927

They did use American Treasury dollars to pay off loans in Wall Street—loans contracted there with private bankers before this country entered the war. That is the explanation of item, "Maturities, $648,246,317", in the summary above.

Item, "Interest, $730,504,177", represents, among other things, the payment of interest on their promissory notes at the United States Treasury with the proceeds of new notes—that is, they borrowed money to pay interest on what they had borrowed before, and continued in a punctilious manner to pay interest in that way, so long as the loans continued; when the Treasury stopped lending they stopped paying interest. Paying interest on borrowed money out of that money itself is under certain temporary circumstances a practice understood by finance; the importance of noting it at all is further to indicate the attitude of the borrowers at the time. The transactions were financial in a strict sense, so understood by every one.

Item, "Reimbursements, $1,872,914,604", represents money borrowed at the United States Treasury by one foreign government to pay back another foreign government. The silver was for India. The other items are generally self-explanatory, with one exception—the largest item of all—namely "Exchange and cotton purchases, $2,644,783,870."

Commenting on this item, the Secretary of the Treasury, annual report 1920, page 71, said: "In the early stages of the war all commodity purchases by Great Britain were thus merged in exchange, except purchases of munitions and sugar. Therefore, the exchange item in the British statement of expenditures reflected purchases of wheat, food, cotton, leather and oil under [British] government control, as well as all transactions of individual buyers in the United States."

Any Treasury statement touching this exchange item, or any banker's statement about it, is bound to be technical, not that the people of finance love to be technical, only that they understand one another better in a language of their own. But what it means is after all quite simple; and it is what Lord Balfour was thinking of when he said to Ambassador Page that the imperative need was for enough American credit to support the exchange—that is to say, the buying power of the pound sterling. Great Britain, remember, had been banker for the Allies since the beginning of the war. Her value to them in that rôle, beyond the fact that she possessed enormous financial resources, was that the pound sterling was the paramount money of the world and that British bankers, from long experience, were the most skillful practitioners of the art of foreign exchange.

Well, what they did here, especially in the "early stages of the war" referred to by the Secretary of the Treasury, meaning early in the period of American participation, was this: Instead of spending the dollars they borrowed out of the American Treasury in a direct manner for American commodities, they spent those dollars to buy the pound sterling (or, as bankers would say, sterling exchange, which comes to the same thing), in the New York exchange market. In one hand they used American Treasury dollars to create British credit with which in the other hand they transacted the business of buying American commodities. But why? Why should they use American dollars to buy sterling exchange, thereby creating British credit to spend, instead of spending American dollars direct for American commodities? Because in that way they could continue to control the international exchange of the world in terms of the pound sterling and uphold the power of British credit. The advantages were very important. For the remainder of the war, the exchange value of the pound sterling, i.e., its buying power, in this country and every other country, was at least one quarter more than its true value; having an unlimited amount of American Treasury dollars to support it with, they were able to "peg" or stabilize it at an artificial value. Thus, wherever in the world the British had to spend pounds they got just that much more for their money. And when the American Government had to buy pounds in London to meet its own war expenses in Great Britain, or to pay the British for transporting American troops to France in British ships, it had to pay just that much more for them and got just that much less for its money. Finally, by thus merging their transactions under the head of exchange, so that they had only to report to the United States Treasury that so and so many dollars had been expended for "exchange", they gained obviously much more freedom of action.

"It will readily be apparent that completely to analyze the total purchases of exchange is impossible."—From the report of the Secretary of the Treasury, 1920, page 72, under the heading, "Expenditures Reported by Foreign Governments."

All the Treasury knew, as the Secretary had said before, was that "the exchange item in the British expenditures reflected purchases of wheat, cotton, leather and oil under [British] Government control, as well as all transactions of individual buyers." Which means that British credit created in the New York foreign exchange market with dollars from the American Treasury was used not only to buy American commodities for the British Government; to an unknown extent it was used also to buy American commodities for British individuals; in other words, for private account as distinct from public account—a distinction modified only by the view that in such a war as that was, all activities, direct and indirect, were vital, even those of private trade. That, indeed, was the view of the United States Treasury, indicated in its popular bulletin on why we were lending the proceeds of Liberty Bonds to foreign governments. In that view it was a question not so much of what they did with the money as how much we could afford to lend.

"Millions of dollars [of Liberty Loan money] were lent to Great Britain after hostilities had ceased to enable her to build up her export trade. There is no question in regard to these facts, and also in regard to the fact that considerable loans were made to the newer countries to help them get on their feet."—From "The Inter-Ally Debts," by Harvey E. Fisk, published by the Bankers Trust Company of New York.

That was quite all right at the time. Whatever the borrowing foreign governments did with their American Treasury dollars was all right, and no question was ever raised about it, so long as they continued to treat the loans in the character in which they were originally understood, meaning loans as such, repayable. But when, after the war, they began to say the only resemblance the loans bore to financial transactions was their legal form, and after they had launched an organized political propaganda, led by the British, for an all-around cancellation of war debts, then the British became extremely resentful of any saying that they had used American Treasury dollars for other than purely war purposes.

On July 14, 1926, Mr. Mellon, then Secretary of the Treasury, wrote a public letter to an American cancellationist to explain, among other things, why in the terms of settlement Great Britain was treated with less leniency than France. In that letter he said: "It must be remembered that England borrowed a large proportion of its debt to us for purely commercial as distinguished from war purposes—to meet its commercial obligations maturing in the United States, to furnish India with silver, to buy food to be resold to its civilian population, and to maintain exchange."

This drew a hot retort from the British Chancellor of the Exchequer, who, on July 19, 1926, rose in Parliament to say:

"During the period of American intervention over seven billions of dollars were spent by Great Britain in the

United States. Of that seven billions we borrowed four and provided an additional three billions from our own independent resources. Regarding commercial maturities, Secretary Mellon must either have been misinterpreted or misled. . . . There has been a great deal of resentment and ill-feeling regarding this debt, and it is very important that this resentment shall not be increased by any misunderstanding of the actual facts."

The next day, July 20, the United States Treasury issued the following statement in rejoinder:

"From England's total reported expenditures in America, from April 6, 1917, to November 1, 1920, there should be deducted the $1,853,000,000 expenditures for which Great Britain was simply the purchasing agent for the other allies and for which Great Britain was paid by the other allies from money loaned to them by the United States. This amount was not provided from England's 'own independent resources.' This leaves $5,366,000,000. Of this amount $1,682,000,000 represents 'exchange and cotton purchases.' The greater part of this expenditure was for the maintenance of sterling exchange, not necessary for purchases in America, but which enabled England to make purchases in other countries at an undepreciated exchange rate. Then $2,643,000,000 was for food and tobacco. A part of this item is probably included in the account out of which England was reimbursed by the other allies, and a part was resold by England to its own civilian population. To the extent of this resale England avoided the necessity of floating loans in its own country. Then $507,877,000 was for interest and principal of England's commercial obligations maturing in America, and $261,000,000 was for silver. The total principal advances to Great Britain after the armistice were $581,000,000."

The British Chancellor of the Exchequer subsided; the next retort came from the British Treasury, not on the facts, but on the interpretation of events. It said:

"Great Britain provided sterling and neutral currencies to meet all her own requirements throughout the war, and in addition, bore the burden of covering the sterling requirements of her continental allies. But for the fact that the United States did not feel able on entering the war to relieve her of that additional burden, Great Britain would have been able to meet from the resources she placed at the disposal of her allies her own expenditures in America, and in all human probability the British debt to the United States would never have been incurred."

What the British Treasury is saying is this—that if only the American Treasury had loaned France, Italy, Belgium and others the money they needed to spend in Great Britain, they would not have had to borrow anything more from Great Britain after we got into the war. They would have had American dollars to spend in Great Britain, and that would have made it very much easier for Great Britain, of course.

III

"The last gasp of repudiation is the plea that under modern democratic conditions no government which depends upon its people for existence and must rely for its continuance in power on reëlection by popular vote can undertake to impose on its people the burden of paying the war debts. I can only comment that if the good faith of governments is to be swallowed up in the bad faith of people, then the world is due for a sad disillusionment."

> —THE HON. BAINBRIDGE COLBY
> Formerly Secretary of State
> in the Wilson Cabinet, speaking against cancellationism,
> April 13, 1932.

"The question of a general joint adjustment of all debts arising out of the war did not arise until after the armistice. It first appears to have been informally suggested by the British Chancellor of the Exchequer to Assistant Secretary of the Treasury Crosby, who was then in Europe, repudiated by him and apparently dropped for the time being."—Annual report of the Secretary of the Treasury, 1920, page 63.

The phrase, "and apparently dropped for the time being", is an example of Treasury accuracy outside of arithmetic. For the debtor governments the situation at that time was extremely delicate. They were politically united against the United States as the great common creditor; the ideal way to make America pay according to her capacity was to involve her at once in a scheme of general war-debt cancellation wherein, as the only ultimate creditor, she would be the only ultimate loser; and it was important to advance immediately upon this object while the American mood was extravagant, and if possible imbed it in the peace treaty. But, on the other hand, they were still borrowing American Treasury dollars on post-armistice account. If they moved too fast, the American Treasury might become suddenly realistic and close the book.

On January 15, 1919, the French High Commissioner in the United States addressed a letter to the Secretary of the Treasury, saying:

"The financial relations among the Allies, brought about by the war, are closely interwoven. The British and French governments have both borrowed from the United States; but France is also a debtor of England. The French and Italian governments have both borrowed from the United States; but Italy is also a debtor of France. Although a debtor of the United States and of Great Britain, France has loaned about 10,000,000,000 francs to its allies. It appears to my government that, if the future adjustment of such mutual accounts is to be made the object of separate and distinct agreements, privileged situations might arise to the prejudice of some of the governments concerned. . . . In short, the French Government looks upon these questions as concerning all the allies and demanding a general and simultaneous settlement."

To this the Secretary of the Treasury replied:

"I agree with you that where two or more of the associated governments have made loans to the same government none should seek any unfair priority or advantage over others in terms of payment, . . . only Great Britain, besides the United States, has made loans to France; and I do not anticipate that the treasuries of the respective countries will have any difficulty in arriving at arrangements which will be equitable and free from discrimination."

A few days later the American Treasury heard that at a meeting of the Financial Drafting Committee appointed by the Council of Ten at the peace conference in Paris the French member, M. Klotz, had supported the proposal that a consolidation and reapportionment of war debts be one of the peace table questions; and the Assistant Secretary of the Treasury in a letter of March 8, 1919, asked the Deputy French High Commissioner in Washington if that was so, saying: "You will appreciate that the Treasury cannot contemplate continuance of advances to any allied government which is lending its support to any plan which would create uncertainty as to its due repayment of advances made to it by the United States Treasury."

The Deputy French High Commissioner replied, saying this had been an Italian proposal in Paris and the French member of the Financial Drafting Committee had been only polite enough not to throw it out of the window. "Furthermore," he said, "with reference to the attitude of the French officials toward the principle involved in this question, the French Government never made any declaration favoring either the Italian proposition or any other similar proposition."

This exchange between the United States Treasury and the Deputy French High Commissioner, in 1919, will be found reprinted in the annual report of the Secretary of the Treasury, year 1926, page 66, together with the following very dry comment:

"It is to be noted that Assistant Secretary Rathbone's letter of March 8, 1919, to Mr. de Billy, Deputy French High Commissioner, stated that the Treasury could not contemplate continuance of advances to any allied government lending its support to a plan which would create uncertainty as to its due repayment of advances made to it by the United States Treasury. Mr. de Billy, in his reply of March 18, 1919, removed this uncertainty as to due repayment. The cash advances of the United States to France subsequent to March 18, 1919, aggregated $690,000,000, and in addition there was an indebtedness of $407,000,000 incurred by France to the United States in the purchase of war stocks, a total of approximately $1,100,000,000."

Nothing more was heard from the French for a long time. From there the British went on with it.

Out of place in the chronology, yet illuminating at this point, are two notable contributions in the American point of view. One is a letter from Norman H. Davis, Assistant Secretary of the Treasury, to President Wilson, dated February 23, 1920 (reprinted in Senate Document Number 86, December 6, 1921), as follows:

"I have for some time suspected that the loans made by England to France and Italy have not the same standing as our loans to the Allies. I recall that Mr. Lloyd George told me England could not afford to force these countries to pay her. Article XI. of the Pact of London states: 'Italy shall receive a military contribution corresponding to her strength and sacrifices.' I do not know what this means. It most probably has a direct relation to the obligations of the Italian Government now held by the British Government, and it may well be that the

British desire a general cancellation of inter-governmental war debts as a means of discharging secret treaty provisions. If such is the case the British might thus in a great part at our expense discharge their treaty obligations."

Another is from the Honorable Oscar F. Crosby, who as Assistant Secretary of the Treasury, had intimate contact with all these matters both here and in Europe. It was he to whom the British Chancellor of the Exchequer first suggested a pooling of war debts. Out of his experiences in Europe Mr. Crosby wrote:

". . . Complex, not simple, relations exist between European countries. Money considerations, territorial transfers, commercial privileges—all these are in constant flux. Among allies, trading is the order of the day. It begins often long before hostilities, continues during the war, is most active at the peace table, and may be protracted during years of adjustment after the war. . . . The money problem between France and Great Britain is only one of many problems arising between them, and it is quite to be expected that France will use every asset, political or material, which may be available in a perfectly legitimate trading process. . . . It is quite possible that while the shuttle is weaving to and fro through these various threads, Great Britain, without waiting for the long-drawn end, may decide to make a gesture of generosity, proposing to cut her claims against France if we will but move *pari passu* with her. . . . And if we decline this sort of proposition, again we play the rôle of the hard-hearted person, etc., to both the British and the French man in the street."

And this turned out to be an amazingly perfect forecast of the celebrated Balfour note, in which the British debt policy has ever since been grounded.

War-debt cancellation became a forbidden subject at the peace conference table; nevertheless, representatives of the British Treasury developed that theme in all the

margins. After the peace conference, on February 4, 1920,
one of them, Mr. Blackett, wrote to the Assistant Secretary of the United States Treasury, saying: ". . . And
as you are aware, the Chancellor of the Exchequer expressed himself ready to take any steps toward relieving
the governments which are debtors to the British Government of the burden of their debts which the United
States Treasury might feel able to propose in regard to
the obligations of the governments which it holds."

Then on February 9, 1920, the British Embassy in
Washington delivered to the American Treasury a message direct from the British Chancellor of the Exchequer
in which he said, flatly: "We should welcome a general
cancellation of intergovernmental war debts."

To this the Secretary of the Treasury, on March 1,
1920, replied in parts as follows:

"Of course I recognize that a general cancellation of
such debts would be of advantage to Great Britain and
that it would probably not involve any losses on her part.
As there are no obligations of the United States Government which would be cancelled under such a plan, the
effect would be that, in consideration of a cancellation by
the United States Government of obligations which it
holds for advances made to the British Government and
other allied governments, the British Government would
cancel its debts against France, Italy, Russia and her
other allies. Such a proposal does not involve mutual
sacrifices on the part of the nations concerned. It simply
involves a contribution mainly by the United States. . . .
A general cancellation as suggested would . . . throw
upon the people of this country the exclusive burden of
meeting the interest and of ultimately extinguishing the
principal of our loans to the allied governments. This
nation has neither sought nor received substantial benefits
from the war. On the other hand, the allies, although
having suffered greatly in loss of lives and property, have,
under the terms of the treaty of peace, and otherwise,

acquired very considerable accessions of territories, populations, economic and other advantages. It would therefore seem that if full account were taken of these and of
the whole situation there would be no desire nor reason
to call upon the government of this country for further
contributions."

Thus the British Treasury came to an impasse with the
American Treasury. Further exchanges were futile. The
next step was much higher. On August 5, 1920, the
Prime Minister of Great Britain, Mr. Lloyd George, wrote
to President Wilson about the debts as follows:

"I come now to the other question I wish to write to
you about, and that is the knotty problem of interallied
indebtedness. . . . The British and French governments
have been discussing during the last four months the question of giving fixity and definiteness to Germany's reparation obligations. The British Government has stood
steadily by the view that it was vital that Germany's
liabilities should be fixed at a figure which it was within
the reasonable capacity of Germany to pay. . . . After
great difficulties with his own people, M. Millerand found
himself able to accept this view, but he pointed out that
it was impossible for France to accept anything less than
it was entitled to under the treaty unless its debts to its
Allies and associates in the war were treated in the same
way. This declaration appeared to the British Government eminently fair. But after careful consideration they
came to the conclusion that it was impossible to remit any
part of what was owed to them by France except as part
and parcel of all-round settlement of interallied indebtedness. . . . Accordingly, the British Government has in-
formed the French Government that it will agree to any
equitable arrangement for the reduction or cancellation of
interallied indebtedness but that such an arrangement
must be one that applies all round. . . . I should very
much welcome any advice which you might feel yourself
able to give me as to the best method of securing that the

whole problem could be considered and settled by the United States Government in concert with its associates."

This is perhaps the most significant one document in the whole record. The word of the British Prime Minister that France will agree to accept reparations in a sum within the reasonable capacity of Germany to pay, only provided the creditors of France forgive France her debts to them; and this seems eminently fair to the British Government, provided the American Government will forgive all of them their debts to the United States Treasury.

President Wilson replied to the Prime Minister of Great Britain as follows, November 3, 1920:

"It is highly improbable that either the Congress or popular opinion in this country will ever permit a cancellation of any part of the debt of the British Government to the United States in order to induce the British Government to remit, in whole or in part, the debt to Great Britain of France or any other of the Allied governments, or that it would consent to a cancellation or reduction in the debts of any of the Allied governments as an inducement towards a practical settlement of the reparation claims. . . . The United States Government . . . fails to perceive the logic in a suggestion in effect either that the United States shall pay part of Germany's reparation obligation or that it shall make a gratuity to the allied governments to induce them to fix such obligation at an amount within Germany's capacity to pay."

President Wilson's letter produced nearly two years of official silence. But in place of all the political and economic arguments that had failed was substituted an emotional propaganda, unprecedented in volume, intensity and ramifications, in the press of Europe, in the press of the United States, in subsidized books, in public and parliamentary speeches, on the American lecture platform by visiting Europeans—all with the effect, if not with the deliberately organized intent, to raise against this country a tide of injurious feeling. This was the Shylock nation, insisting upon the value of its dollars against the lives Europe had poured out in a common cause. And all this time Europe's promissory notes lay fading in the vaults of the United States Treasury. The debtor governments ignored them. They had not been funded into long-term bonds, as the contract was; not a dollar of interest had been paid.

Suddenly, in July, 1922, all the anti-American feeling thus prepared in Europe was gathered up and fixed in the famous Balfour note, which for both literary style and subtlety of dialect is one of the fine examples of demagogic statescraft in the political papers of the English language.

Lord Balfour was then Acting Secretary of State for Foreign Affairs. He addressed his note to France and then separately to each of Great Britain's debtors. The policy favored by the government of Great Britain, he said to them, was "that of surrendering their share of German reparations and writing off through one great transaction the whole body of inter-allied indebtedness." Now, with "the greatest reluctance", with "distaste", Great Britain was obliged to adopt another policy, and the reason for this was that the American Government was demanding the payment of Great Britain's debt to the United States Treasury. Thus, Great Britain was "regretfully constrained" to ask her debtors to pay, but the amount she would ask them to pay would depend not on what they owed Great Britain but on what Great Britain would have to pay America.

"In no circumstances," said Lord Balfour, "do we propose to ask more from our debtors than is necessary to pay our creditors, and while we do not ask for more, all will admit that we can hardly be content with less, for it should not be forgotten, though it sometimes is, that our liabilities were incurred for others, not for ourselves."

Then he explained why it had been necessary for Great Britain to incur its debt to the United States Treasury for others, not for itself. The reason was that "the United

States insisted, in substance if not in form, that though our allies were to spend the money it was only on our security that they were prepared to lend it."

Thus was it laid eminently upon the mind of Europe that there would be no reparations for Germany to pay, no war debts for one government to pay another, but for the fact that the American Government was demanding its war dollars back; and laid at the same time upon the mind of England that the entire British debt to the United States Treasury arose from the fact that the American Government during the war had been willing to lend its dollars to the Allies only on the guarantee of Great Britain.

The American reaction to the Balfour note was one of deep astonishment. The American Ambassador to Great Britain in a speech at the Pilgrim's Dinner said he did not doubt that the British Government itself would remove the misapprehensions created by Lord Balfour. The British Government was silent. But Lord Balfour replied to the American Ambassador in a public statement, in which he said:

"The American Ambassador, as I understand it, regards the financial arrangements between partners in the great war as so many isolated undertakings to be separately considered and carried through one by one. . . . I am myself inclined to a somewhat less commercial view. . . . I do not propose to criticise those who differ from me, but one final observation I will make on this matter. If, as I suppose, it is the first of these competing views which commends itself to public opinion in the United States, the unconditional and uncontested legal rights of that country could not have been enforced in a manner less likely to injure the happy relations which I am glad to say prevail between the two peoples."

As for Lord Balfour's statement that Great Britain's debt to the American Treasury was incurred for others, not for itself—this is merely a refinement returned upon the British Treasury's original thesis, namely, that if the American Treasury had loaned France, Italy, Belgium and others all the dollars needed to meet their expenditures in Great Britain, then it would not have been necessary for them to borrow anything more from Great Britain; they would have been able, instead, to buy in Great Britain with American dollars and Great Britain would have had more dollars to spend in the United States.

In a statement to the Associated Press, March 9, 1923, the Honorable Oscar T. Crosby, Assistant Secretary of the Treasury during the war, said: "Lord Balfour says: 'We explained to the American Government that we should be able to find all the dollars necessary to purchase our own war materials without borrowing from the United States or anybody else.' Certainly no such statement came to my knowledge. On the contrary, the need of borrowing dollars for British requirements here (and even in neutral countries) was always in the forefront in my contact with the subject."

Then as concerning Lord Balfour's statement that "the United States insisted, in substance if not in form, that although our allies were to spend the money it was only on our security they were prepared to lend it",—simply, it was not so. The record says it was not so. Every Secretary of the Treasury, then and since, has said it was not so. The policy of the United States Treasury was to make loans to foreign governments separately, to each on its own security. This was explicit. Lord Balfour himself must have forgotten that eighteen months before he wrote this misapprehension into his celebrated note, the British Chancellor of the Exchequer, rising to an interrogation in the House of Commons (February 22, 1921), declared: "No loan made by the United States Government to allied governments was ever guaranteed by us."

The *London Economist,* which ranks first in Great Britain if not in the world among economic journals, had the gaunt and solitary honesty, (February 14, 1925), to say: "The Balfour note endeavours to create the impression that our payment to America is not part of the war costs chargeable against Great Britain at all, and does so by making two false suggestions. The first is that our borrowings in America were not for our own use, when, in fact, they were largely spent upon feeding our own people; the second is that America, unwilling to lend to our Allies, handed the money to us to pass on to them, whereas, in fact, the United States was lending to the European Allies £1,315 millions while she was lending Great Britain £940 millions. . . . There is no special characteristic of our American debt that differentiates it from other war costs."

But the emotional power of the Balfour note was terrific. If he was contemptuous of facts, he was even more contemptuous of money and exchange, and of consistency, too, for this was the same Arthur James Balfour who had said to Ambassador Page in 1917 that what they most needed was enough American credit to support the British exchange. Now, when it is all over, as Lord Balfour, Acting Secretary of State for Foreign Affairs, he says:

"It is true that many of the Allied and associated powers are as between each other creditors or debtors or both, but they were and are much more. They were partners in the greatest international effort ever made in the cause of freedom and they still are partners in dealing with some at least of its results. Their debts were incurred, their loans were made, not for the separate advantage of particular states, but for the great purpose common to them all, and that purpose has been in the main accomplished.

"To generous minds it can never be agreeable, although for reasons of state it may perhaps be necessary, to regard the monetary aspect of this great event as a thing apart, to be torn from its historical setting and treated as no more than ordinary commercial dealing between traders who borrow and capitalists who lend."

This passage had endless reverberations in this country; and then when British publicists began to orchestrate the Balfour theme with variations such as this from the brilliant J. M. Keynes—

> So long as America was sending materials and munitions to be used by Allied soldiers, she charged us for them and these charges are the origin of what we now owe her. But when later on she sent men, too, to use the munitions themselves, then we were charged nothing. Evidently there is not much logic in a system which causes us to owe money to America, not because she was able to help us so much but because at first she was able to help us, so far at least as man power was concerned, so little.

—there were many Americans, some unfamiliar with the facts, on whom the impression was the effect intended.

Indeed, the one valid ground, if any, on which to cancel war debts all around, would be that it was a common cause in principle as represented in Lord Balfour's exalted language, a cause above money, above spoils, above advantage, then and afterward, and that it was so treated by all the nations engaged, save only the United States. In that case we should be ashamed. But was it in that case?

"Until the war ended no intimation was made that these advances were subsidies, or that they were contributions to a joint cause, or that they would be the subject of a general pooling after the war."—Secretary of the Treasury, under the heading, "Obligations of Foreign Governments", annual report 1926, page 60.

During the war, for obvious reasons, the Allies found it necessary to make large expenditures in the countries of one another. Before we entered the conflict, the rule among them was that so far as possible each one loaned the others the money the others needed to spend in its own country.

Thus, England loaned her allies the pounds sterling to meet their expenditures in the British Empire, France loaned her allies the francs they needed to meet their expenditures in France, and so on. The result would be that after the war all would have claims against one another for money so loaned; then claims would cancel claims, by a simple clearing of credits and debits, leaving only the net balances to be considered.

When we entered the war the United States Treasury embraced that principle. It undertook to lend the Allies all the dollars they needed to spend for food, munitions, supplies and services in this country. But, on the other hand, the Allies never extended that principle to us. To meet our own war expenditures in the British Empire we were obliged to buy pounds sterling, and we paid for them in cash. To meet American war expenditures in France, which were enormous, the United States Treasury was obliged to buy francs, and it paid for them in cash. The same in Italy; the same everywhere. The United States was lending dollars to Great Britain, France, Italy and others to meet their expenditures in the United States and at the same time buying for cash the pounds sterling, the francs, the lire, etc., to meet our own expenditures in those countries. Moreover, the cost to us of those pounds and francs, etc., was greater because in the New York Exchange market the British were using dollars out of the American Treasury to hold the pound sterling at an artificial value; and the French on a smaller scale were doing the same thing with the franc.

"For its own purposes in Great Britain, France and Italy the United States did not borrow pounds or francs or lire. Our Treasury was obliged to procure these currencies for the use of our Army abroad. We bought pounds, francs and lire from the governments of Great Britain, France and Italy and made payment therefor in dollars here."—Assistant Secretary of the Treasury Rathbone, annual report of the Treasury, 1926, page 61.

"We purchased supplies and services from France and the British Empire by hundreds of millions. They had to be paid for in francs and in pounds. We did not get those francs and pounds on credit; we paid cash for them. . . . In other words, we paid cash for the goods and services necessary to enable us to make our joint contribution to the common cause. Our associates got the goods and services purchased in this country to enable them to make that part of their joint contribution on credit. Here is the fundamental reason which explains why we ended the war with every one owing us and our owing no one. We are now urged to cancel these debts because it is alleged that they were incurred in a common cause. Neither abroad nor in this country has it been suggested that if this is to be done, we are to be reimbursed the dollars actually expended by us in France and Great Britain, so that the goods and services they sold to us might constitute their contribution to the common cause. . . . Among the purposes for which we made dollar advances was that of maintaining the franc and the pound at somewhere near their normal values. In other words, we loaned our associates the dollars with which to purchase bills on London and Paris and so permit them to peg the exchanges. When we were obliged to buy francs and sterling for our own uses in the Paris and London markets we did so at the artificial prices maintained by the use of the very funds we had loaned."—From a letter by the Secretary of the Treasury, Mr. Mellon, to certain Princeton Professors, March 15, 1927.

It has still to be mentioned that the goods and services bought in this country with borrowed dollars by the Allies were bought at controlled prices. They paid only what the American Government paid for like goods and services. But the goods and services bought by the American Government in allied countries for cash were bought at uncontrolled or civilian prices.

There is a kind of indecent plausibility in saying that

when we sent supplies and ammunitions to the Allies we charged for them, whereas when we sent man power to consume our own supplies and ammunition we charged nothing, so that now when we talk of collecting a debt owing us for supplies and ammunition, we seem to be setting a value upon things over the value of the lives we ourselves were willing to contribute.

When we began to send man power into the allied countries—no, we did not charge for that. We were charged for it.

We were charged for moving American soldiers across the sea in British ships; we bought pounds sterling with dollars and paid cash for that British service. We were charged port dues for landing ships in French harbors —ships bearing our own munitions and supplies; we bought French francs with dollars and paid cash for the right to enter. We were charged for moving American soldiers, American munitions and American supplies on French railroads to the front; we bought francs with dollars and paid cash for the privilege of getting our man power and equipment to where the war was. Everything the Allies got in this country they borrowed; for everything we got in the allied countries we paid cash. Never through all the tumult about war debts has this detail of truth been mentioned by the allied governments to us, nor by any of them to their own people.

Where was Lord Balfour's common cause, above money or advantage? Where was it among the Allies themselves? The peace conference was a terrific struggle for advantage. The English thought France got it.

Certainly ideas of separate advantage in a very ancient sense governed the Allies when they were dividing among themselves by trade and barter more than a million square miles of former German territory in Asia and Africa and all the property of both the German Government and its nationals that was lying about the world, and then islands of strategic importance in the Pacific which naturally belonged to the naval frontier of this country. None of this we touched. But when, after rejecting the Treaty of Versailles, we had made a separate peace with Germany and appeared with certain claims against her for specific damage to persons and property, such, for example, as claims arising from the *Lusitania* case, the Allies took the position that we could not collect anything from Germany because their claims upon her for more reparations than she could pay had priority over any claims of ours.

IV

As concerning payment, the dollars left in Europe by American tourists in one average year would much more than pay Europe's total annual obligation to the United States Treasury.
—DATA FROM THE DEPARTMENT OF COMMERCE

The American Treasury closed its till to foreign governments in November, 1920, more than two years after the armistice. The last advance was one of $10,000,000 to France. But that was not the end of foreign borrowing. The foreign governments turned from the American Treasury to Wall Street and began to borrow there out of the private American reservoir. Their access to it was very free. They borrowed in Wall Street, on their bonds, for every conceivable purpose—for public works, for reconstruction, to avoid increasing taxation at home, to postpone balancing their budgets and to support their inflated currencies.

At this point the remnants of rationality appear to depart. Those who denounce America as a Shylock nation because we expect them to honor their debts to the American Treasury are at the same time borrowing more and more American capital in Wall Street! And this was the beginning of those enormous private loans to Europe which became in a few years so large that Europe could say, which now she is saying: "We cannot pay both our private debt to the United States Treasury and our debt to the American investor. Which will America have?"

Before the public till had been closed to foreign governments the Secretary of the Treasury, in a letter to the British Chancellor of the Exchequer, March 8, 1920, had said: "Since the armistice this government has extended to foreign governments financial assistance to the extent of approximately four billions of dollars. What this government could do for the immediate relief of the debtor countries has been done. Their need now is for private credits. The indebtedness of the allied governments to each other and to the United States is not a present burden upon the debtor governments, since they are not paying interest, or even, as far as I am aware, providing in their budgets for the payment of either principal or interest."

Then at last, when it had cut them off, the American Treasury declared a three-year moratorium on their obligations and reminded them of their undertaking, on the request of the Secretary of the Treasury, to convert their hasty promissory notes into long-term bonds parallel to the Liberty Bonds the American Government had sold to raise the money. The only response to this reminder was the onset of that propaganda for debt cancellation which crystallized itself in the Balfour note.

For a year after the Balfour note nothing new happened, except that Reginald McKenna, a former Chancellor of the British Exchequer, came before the American Bankers' Convention in New York with the unexpected thesis that the war debts were beyond the capacity of any debtor country to pay, Great Britain alone excepted. She could pay; in her accumulated foreign investments she had adequate resources out of which to discharge her debt to the United States Treasury. But that was not the point. If all the debtor countries could afford to pay as well as Great Britain, still the United States could not afford to receive payment, because, of course, she would have to receive payment in foreign goods and such enormous payments in the shape of foreign goods would ruin American industries.

That idea, too, like all European ideas, found fertile ground to fall upon; and although the area was not large, the intensive cultivation of it brought forth from this seed a very large crop. We have never since been rid of the curious fallacy that a creditor nation in our case cannot afford to receive payment. The argument has become familiar. The principal of great debts cannot be paid in gold; in the whole world there is not enough gold for that purpose, and, besides, that is not what gold is for. Therefore, debtor nations must pay their debts in goods. But since we set tariff barriers against the incoming of foreign goods, and do this because we are in the manufacturing business ourselves, how can we expect our debtors to pay us in goods? If there were no tariff barriers, they might be able to pay us in goods, but that would only invert the problem, for to receive the goods would ruin our own industries.

A more muddled argument was never imagined. Our debtors cannot pay unless we remove our tariff barriers. It stands thus on a free-trade leg. But if we remove the tariff barriers and let them pay, our unprotected industries will be ruined. It stands then on the leg of high protection. Perceive that if this were sound as a proposition in economics it would have to hold for the payment of international debts in principle, not war debts only; and that if it does so hold in principle, international debts as such are reduced to a logical absurdity. But to save the reason it is necessary only to set an adjective before the word goods.

It may be true, probably is true, that a nation in our case, or in England's case, cannot afford to receive payment in competitive goods. The illuminating fact is that only about four tenths of the international trade of the world runs in competitive goods; the other six tenths is in noncompetitive goods, the exchange of which may be increased to any degree with mutual benefit. England is the great creditor nation. Her foreign investments are much larger and older than ours. She has never discovered any logical difficulty about receiving payment from her debtors. She was for a long time a free-trade nation, with no tariffs against foreign goods because her industry at first and for a long time was without any effective competition in the world. Her debtors did not pay her in cutlery such as she made herself at Sheffield, nor in textiles such as were made at Manchester, nor in coal, of which she had a surplus; but she was very willing to receive payment in such commodities as iron ore, raw cotton, raw wool, hides and wheat. Conditions have changed. English industry now demands protection against competitive foreign goods. So the theory of free trade is abandoned; British tariffs, like American tariffs, begin to rise, and yet you will not hear British bankers saying that for this reason Great Britain's debtors will be unable to pay her, or that Great Britain cannot afford to receive payment.

Say that we could not afford to receive payment from Great Britain in motor cars. That may be quite true. It would injure our motor-car industry, provided British motor cars were cheaper than ours. But we are quite willing to receive payment in British tin, of which we have no source of our own, in British rubber, in British jute, and so on. Moreover, there are immense triangular transactions in foreign trade, as when Great Britain sells motor cars in Brazil and Brazil sells coffee in the United States. Brazil settles with Great Britain for the motor cars with a coffee credit in New York; and Great Britain, if she likes, may use that coffee credit to pay an instalment of her debt to the United States Treasury. The only sense in what Mr. McKenna said to the American bankers was this,—that a creditor nation will not be benefited by receiving payment from its debtors in goods it does not want. That was, after all, not a very startling idea; it failed perceptibly to advance the European cause of debt cancellation.

So in 1923 the British Government sent a mission to Washington to settle Great Britain's debt. It was settled for eighty cents on the dollar. This was the first and highest of the principal settlements.

And it was made with the World War Foreign Debt Commission. This was a body that had been created by Congress to settle with the debtor countries, according to the capacity of each one to pay, not according to the contract. On January 4, 1926, the Secretary of the Treasury, speaking as chairman of the Debt Commission, made the following statement to the Ways and Means Committee of Congress on the settlements in general and the Anglo-American agreement in particular:

"Since foreign debt settlements do not seem to be clearly understood, I wish to mention some rather elemental facts. The obligations held by the Treasury [the original promissory notes of the foreign borrowers] generally call for payment on demand, and such payment cannot be made. We must find practical terms. Now, if we are owed $62 and payment is made to-day we receive the full value of our loan. If payment is made at the rate of $1 a year for 62 years without interest we would be conceding a part of the debt. What this concession amounts to can be variously estimated depending on the rate of discount arbitrarily taken. If we used $4\frac{1}{4}$ per cent., the present value of a $1 annuity for 62 years is a little over $21; if we use 3 per cent. its present value is $28. If, however, instead of $1 a year for 62 years without interest we should charge interest at the cost of money to us, we get the full value of the loan, since we could borrow the $62 to-day, pay interest on the borrowing, and repay the principal as annuities are received. From the United States standpoint, therefore, the question of whether a particular settlement represents a reduction in the debt depends on whether the interest charged over the entire period of the agreement is less than the average cost to us of money during that period. The flexibility in debt settlements is found in the rate of interest to be charged. . . .

"Great Britain was the first nation to recognize the desirability of putting its house in order. Great Britain owed us some $4,600,000,000 of principal and interest on its demand obligations. The American Debt Commission recommended a settlement on the basis of principal payments over a 62-year period, with interest at the rate of 3 per cent. per annum for the first 10 years and $3\frac{1}{2}$ per cent. thereafter. Congress has approved the settlement. Taking into account the current interest rate when the settlement was made, the British agreement does not represent payment in full. If we figure the present value of the settlement at $4\frac{1}{4}$ per cent. we cancelled 20 per cent. of the debt. The settlement, however, was entirely based on our estimation of Great Britain's capacity to pay. It is a precedent for the recognition of the principle of capacity to pay and is not a set formula to control other cases of substantially less capacity."

Finland was the very first to settle; but she was in the class of post-armistice borrowers only. Of the principal debtors Great Britain was the first to settle. Her anxiety was to restore the pound sterling to a gold basis; and for that purpose, after having made terms with the American Treasury, she borrowed $300,000,000 gold in Wall Street.

"The largest banking credit ever formed for the benefit and use of a foreign nation during peace times was established yesterday in New York. It was $300,000,000, or three times the amount of the Bank of France credit set up one year ago. Of this British credit, $200,000,000 was taken by the Federal Reserve Bank and $100,000,000 by the private banking firm of J. P. Morgan and Company. Both items in this credit were arranged for the Bank of England and through it for the British Government. The purpose was to facilitate Great Britain's return to a gold basis. . . . Sympathy will be shown by this government

to any effort to aid the British Government in its attempt
to keep its currency at par. It is understood here that purchases by the New York Federal Reserve Bank of sterling on the open market will receive Treasury approval."
—*New York Times,* April 29, 1925.

On the day before, the British Chancellor of the Exchequer, in a budget speech before the House of Commons, said:

"Finally, although we believe we are strong enough to
achieve this important change from our new resources,
and as a further precaution to make assurance doubly
sure, I have made arrangements to obtain, if required,
credits in the United States of not less than $300,000,000,
with the possibility of expansion if need be. . . . These
great credits across the Atlantic Ocean have been obtained and built up as a solemn warning to speculators
of every kind and in every country of the resistance which
they will encounter and of the reserves with which they
will be confronted if they attempt to disturb the gold
parity which Great Britain has now established."
[Cheers.]

For two years more the other principal debtors, France,
Italy and Belgium, continued to ignore the existence of
the World War Foreign Debt Commission in Washington, continued to ignore their promissory notes in the
vaults of the American Treasury, continued also to borrow heavily in Wall Street out of the private American
reservoir.

Then—

"As a matter of administrative policy it was determined to deny recourse to our money market by the debtor
nations or their nationals until the nation negotiated a
settlement of its debt to the United States."—From a
letter by the Secretary of the Treasury to the President,
annual Treasury report, 1926, page 214.

This is to say, the American Government announced
that a foreign government refusing to recognize its debt

to the American Treasury should no longer have access
to the private American reservoir, neither that government
nor its nationals. After this, if they came to Wall Street
seeking new loans, Wall Street was obliged to say to them:
"Sorry, but you will have to see the United States
Treasury first."

That brought them all to Washington, and for the next
two years the Debt Commission was very busy. As they
settled with the American Treasury the ban was lifted and
they resumed their borrowing in Wall Street. Italy, on her
way home from Washington, where she had settled with
the Treasury for twenty-six cents on the dollar, stopped in
Wall Street and borrowed $100,000,000 at the market
price. The last debtor but one to settle was France, in
1926. The very last was Yugoslavia.

No debtor settled in full. In each case the debtor laid
before the Debt Commission a statement of its condition
and resources and the Debt Commission, in collaboration
with the debtor, thereby arrived at an estimate of what it
could pay. There was a fiction in each case that the debtor
should be able to say it had discharged the principal in
full, and for that reason the sixty-two graduated annual
payments, beginning small, were in an arbitrary manner
divided between principal and interest—the interest very
low or nominal—in order that the column showing payments of principal might add up to the full amount. But
in every case the cost to the American Treasury of the
money raised for these loans by the sale of Liberty Bonds
was more than the rate of interest charged in the settlements. The rough result of the principal settlements, that
with England alone excepted, was that we should get back
in full with interest only what we had loaned after the
armistice.

"Let us see what relation the burden of our debt settlements bears to our loans after the armistice. . . . In the
case of England, post-armistice advances with interest
amounted to $660,000,000, and the present value of the

entire debt settlement is $3,297,000,000. It must be re-membered that England borrowed a large proportion of its debt to us for purely commercial as distinguished from war purposes.

"France's after-the-war indebtedness with interest amounts to $1,655,000,000. The settlement negotiated by Ambassador Bérenger with the American Debt Funding Commission has a present value of $1,681,000,000.

"Belgium's post-armistice borrowings with interest were $258,000,000, and the present value of the settlement is $192,000,000.

"With Italy the situation is similar. Its post-armistice indebtedness with interest is $800,000,000 and the present value of its debt settlement is $426,000,000. It is the same as regards Serbia."—Secretary of the Treasury, annual report 1926, page 261.

Given a rate of interest, the present or cash value of a series of annuities is an actuarial finding. It can no more be disputed than the table of interest. Present value, as used by the Secretary of the Treasury above, means simply the value of these settlements in the impossible case that the American Treasury could have found some one to take all those funded foreign government obligations off its hands for cash—some imaginary investor with that sum of money to invest, who could believe the instalments would be paid to the end in punctual manner and that $4\frac{1}{4}$ per cent. was a fair rate of interest for sixty-two years. On that basis of calculation you could say that Great Britain settled for eighty cents on the dollar, France for fifty cents and Italy for twenty-six cents.

The settlements were criticized, by some on the ground that they were too lenient, by others on the ground that they were too hard, and by others on the ground that they were unequal. The cancellationists were most vocal, say-ing the settlements were too hard.

"It is assumed that generosity did not enter into the negotiations of the Commission. It certainly was very lenient to Italy and it cannot be condemned as harsh to France when there is imposed no greater burden on that nation than the collection of the post-armistice indebtedness at five per cent. interest. French papers admit the Franco-British settlement, all things considered, is much more burdensome than the Franco-American settlement. No test of generosity is set up by the Columbia professors, but it is just assumed America was ungenerous.

"The Columbia professors complain because all debtors were not treated on an equality. They speak of a settlement of eighty per cent. present value with Great Britain and twenty-six per cent. present value with Italy. Do they propose to correct this want of equality by raising the Italian settlement to that of the British, which of course would impose a burden impossible of performance by Italy, or do they propose that the British be reduced to fifty per cent. and the Italian raised to fifty per cent., which would make an easy settlement for Great Britain and still an impossible settlement for Italy, or do they propose that the British settlement shall be brought down to the Italian twenty-six per cent., thus imposing no real burden on England at all? If the last is their proposition, then why cannot Italy say its twenty-six per cent. should be reduced to zero, because we are collecting nothing from another debtor, as, for instance, Armenia?"—From a letter by Senator Smoot, a member of the World War Foreign Debt Commission, to certain Columbia professors, December 20, 1926.

Then after all, the settlements settled nothing. European invective against this country for wanting its war dollars back went on as before; it never for one day ceased. The only change was one of tense. Before the settlements, it was that Europe would be ruined if she had to pay; afterward, as payments began to be made, the ruin of Europe was taking place.

It was with the assistance of American credit in Wall Street that Great Britain in 1925 restored the pound sterling to the gold basis. "By bringing sterling exchange to parity," said Senator Smoot, chairman of the Senate Finance Committee, "England in paying its adverse international trade balance saves each year more than the annuity on the American debt."

Nevertheless, within a year from the date of the budget speech in which he had referred so dramatically to the use and value of "those great credits across the Atlantic", the British Chancellor of the Exchequer rose again in the House of Commons and said this gratuitous thing:

"When France and Italy have funded their debts, both to this country and to the United States, and when other minor powers have funded their debts, it is clear that the United States will be receiving, directly and indirectly, on her own account from reparations, from Italian sources balanced against reparations, from British sources, from French sources through British hands and from Italian sources through British hands, by far the larger part, at least sixty per cent., of the total probable reparations of Germany. An extraordinary situation will be developed, that by all these chains and lines and channels, the pressure of debt extraction will draw reparations from the devastated and war-stricken countries of Europe, and they will pass in an unbroken stream across the Atlantic to that wealthy and prosperous and great Republic. These facts will not pass out of the minds of any responsible persons either in the United States or Europe."

This picture of wealth flowing in an unbroken stream from war-stricken Europe to America was utterly false.

As the British Chancellor was speaking, and as he must have known, the situation was that for each dollar received by the American Treasury on account of war debts Wall Street was lending three in Europe. The stream was heavily the other way. The situation was—and everybody knew it—that Germany was paying reparations with money that flowed first from the United States to Germany. American loans to Germany alone, out of the private American reservoir, to enable her to pay reparations to France, England, Italy, Belgium and others—our loans to Germany alone have amounted to more than twice the total amount received so far by the American Treasury from England, France, Italy, Belgium and others on account of their war-debt settlements. And yet the British Chancellor of the Exchequer might lay upon the imagination of the world the hateful suggestion that this country was drawing reparations from the devastated and war-stricken countries of Europe!

Such are the distortions, like acids, that produce the chemistries of European hatred to which so many Americans react by saying: "Right or wrong we cannot afford to collect the war debts. There will be too much bad feeling about it." That is only to say, we must buy the good will of Europe. Then what a joke it would be on us if it should turn out that the war debts were a pretext only.

"Finally, the joint faculties of Columbia and Princeton urge the American people to reconsider the debt schemes with the allied countries 'because of the growing odium with which this country is coming to be regarded by our European associates.' I doubt whether European nations dislike us as much as some people tell us they do. But I know this, that if they do, the cancellation of that part of their debt which has not already been cancelled will not of itself change their dislike into affection. Neither in international relations any more than in private life is affection a purchasable commodity, while my observation and reading of history lead me to conclude that a nation is hardly likely to deserve and maintain the respect of other nations by sacrificing its own just claims."—From a letter by the Secretary of the Treasury, Mr. Mellon, to certain Princeton professors, March 15, 1927.

The subject entire becomes at length so irrationalized by political misrepresentation in the Old World manner, by the dread of Americans to be thought ill of in Europe, and by the divided utterances of those in this country whose interest in private loans to Europe may cause them secretly to wish for a cancellation of war debts at the expense of the American taxpayer, that scarcely any popular assumption about it is within the perspective of fact, and the facts themselves become incredible. Certainly many Americans assume that the burden of war debt payments has been heavy on the debtor countries. But this burden—what is the measure of it?

"The British settlement calls for an average annual charge corresponding to 1.9 per cent. of the total British foreign trade, the Belgian settlement 0.88 per cent., the Italian settlement 2.87 per cent., and the French settlement 2.64 per cent. Great Britain's average annuity represents 0.94 per cent. of its national income, Belgium's 0.8 per cent., Italy's 0.97 per cent., France's 1.47 per cent."—Statement of the Secretary of the Treasury before the Ways and Means Committee of Congress, May 20, 1926.

That was the case in 1926. All the percentages afterward fell, because both Europe's foreign trade and the national income of the principal European countries increased. They would be somewhat different now in a state of world-wide depression, but abnormally different. The depression is abnormal.

The average total receipts of the American Treasury from the European debt settlements in the first five years was $213,523,120. In the year 1931, but for the moratorium, it would have been roughly $250,000,000. The crushing effects of this sum upon Europe is of course imaginary. For Great Britain, less than $165,000,000; for France, less than $40,000,000; for Italy, less than $15,000,000; for Belgium, less than $7,500,000; for Poland, less than $6,500,000; and then on down the scale. Great Britain the most, as her capacity is. For Great Britain, however, it is hardly more than one tenth of her own income from foreign investments. Say it is $3.50 per capita for war-debt payments to the American Treasury. In 1928 Great Britain's annual income from foreign investments was $29.00 per capita. (Memorandum on International Trade and Balances of Payments, League of Nations, 1927-1929, Volume II.)

There are other measures.

The cash value of the British settlement with the American Treasury in 1923 was a little more than 3¼ billions of dollars. Since then the new capital issues for foreign countries on the London money market have amounted to 4½ billions. (Figures from the Midland Bank, Ltd., London.) Since assuming the burden of war-debt payments Great Britain has increased her own foreign investments by more than the cash value of her settlement with the American Treasury.

The cash value of the French settlement with the American Treasury in 1926 was $1,655,000,000. (Annual report of the Treasury, 1926, page 261.) Since then the gold holdings of the Bank of France have increased $2,-000,000,000. That is to say, the increase alone in the gold holdings of the Bank of France since the settlement of the French war debt with the American Treasury is $345,-000,000 more than the cash value of that settlement at the time it was made. In 1931 the Bank of France had gold balances in New York equal to one half the entire principal cash value of her war debt to the United States Treasury.

One of the consequences of settling with the debtor countries on the capacity of each one to pay, not on the written contract, was that in negotiating their agreements they made of course in every case a statement of poverty. It would be only human. They were trading. The more convincing a statement of poverty was, the better the trade one could make with the American Debt Commission. This was understood. The Debt Commission checked their statements so far as possible; but after all, what you know about another country's economics you take from its own figures. And always those statements of poverty were reinforced by propaganda in the

American and European press and in speeches on every international occasion. More or less exaggeration was unavoidable. Moreover, everybody at that time inclined to underestimate the recuperative power of the world. Much of this power was new, comparable only to the amazing power of destruction developed for the war. Power of the same kind, now turned to reconstruction.

The poverty of Europe to-day is either political and imaginary, like the crushing effect of the war debt to the American Treasury, or an idea derived from envious comparison with the United States. In its own world Europe is richer than ever before. The standard of living is higher than before the war, so much higher that a return to pre-war conditions is unimaginable. France is richer in gold. Great Britain is richer in investments. The whole of Europe is richer in material power and equipment, in all the means to the production of wealth.

"The year 1925 marks in some respects a turning point in post-war economic developments. Europe's production probably reached the pre-war level in this year; and the quantum of world trade was for the first time greater than in 1913. . . . The adjustment which had taken place laid the foundation for a striking economic progress in the quinquennium 1925-1929, which is illustrated by the following chart:

NATIONAL INDICES OF INDUSTRIAL PRODUCTION

(Base: 1925 equals 100)

Country	1926	1927	1928	1929
France	116	102	119	130
Germany	95	120	120	122
Poland	98	123	138	138
United Kingdom	77	111	105	113
United States	104	102	107	114

"The main impetus to economic activity after 1925 came from an extraordinary advance in industrial technique and management—rationalization—in agriculture as well as in manufacturing industries. Equally important perhaps was the improvement in the means of communication and transit due to the increased use of motor vehicles and electricity. Finally, almost all countries gradually stabilized their currencies; and international lending on a commercial basis reached large dimensions.

"This progress was of course far from being either general or uniform. It was much more vigorous in Europe than in other continents. Between 1925 and 1929 the aggregate production of crude products in Europe advanced nearly 4½ per cent. per annum, while the average annual increase in all other continents taken together was less than 2¼ per cent. Even these figures understate the case; for, in the basic year 1925, the European harvests happened to be exceptionally good. Thus, by 1929, Europe had recovered the ground lost in preceding years and the pre-war equilibrium between Europe and the rest of the world had been very largely restored."— From Course and Phases of the World Economic Depression, League of Nations, 1931.

And lastly, until the moratorium of war-debt payments declared on the initiative of this country last year for the ease of our European debtors—until then, the burden of payment on their settlements with the American Treasury had never touched them really. The explanation is that new loans to the same countries out of the private American reservoir greatly exceeded their payments to the American Treasury. Much faster than they paid money into the American Treasury they borrowed it again in Wall Street. And in the normal course of events this might go on and on without end, for naturally American loans to Europe would increase more each year than the sum of European payments to the American Treasury on account of war debts, so that, in fact, the burden of payment need never touch them at all.

It is not the burden, in size or shape. The impasse is mental. To comprehend it one must reckon with the ways of Old World diplomacy, its passion for manipulations, its elaborate involutions of policy, the reach of its scheming. All its political arrangements are complex; all its bargains are compound. It knows no simple realities.

We think of the war debts as if they concerned only the American Treasury on this side and the separate debtor nations on the other side. We insist they are not political. Nevertheless, they have become involved in the political bargains of Europe. There is, for example, a bargain of record between our principal debtors on one hand and Germany on the other as to how any further cancellation of European debts owing to the American Treasury shall be divided among them. This bargain is Article 2 of "Special Memorandum" in the Young Plan, called in English, "Report of the Committee of Experts on Reparations", printed by His Majesty's Stationer, London, June, 1919, and reads as follows:

"2. Any relief which any Creditor Power may effectively receive, in respect of its net outward payments on account of War Debts; after making due allowance for any material or financial counter-considerations, and after taking into account any remissions on account of war-debt receipts which it may itself make, shall be dealt with as follows:

"As regards the first 37 years—

"(a) Germany shall benefit to the extent of two-thirds of the net relief available, by way of a reduction in her annuity obligations thereafter.

"(b) One-third of the net relief shall be retained by the creditor concerned."

That is to say, if the American Government reduces or cancels the remainder of the European war debts, two thirds of the benefit shall pass to Germany in remission of reparations and one third shall be retained; or, for each dollar of war debts we forgive our debtors they will

forgive Germany 66⅔ cents. How that interesting division
was arrived at or what bargains off the record underlie
this one, we do not know.

V

It is a fraud to accept what you cannot repay.
—PUBLILIUS SYRUS

The celebrated Balfour note, so unfair to this country,
was a powerful two-edged stroke in European diplomacy,
and it was, no doubt, more significant in that aspect
than from any resentful American point of view. When
the British Chancellor of the Exchequer makes a speech
on war debts, as to say, for example, that the United
States is drawing reparations from the devastated and
war-stricken countries of Europe, we read it for direct
meaning, but France reads it for its indirect political
meaning. Is England inclining a little more to Germany?
And as her conclusion may be as to that, so France may
alter her tone with Germany. There is a British policy
with France and a British policy with Germany, a French
policy with Great Britain and a French policy with Germany, a German policy toward each of these, and so on;
and in all of these more or less Europe's war debts to the
American Treasury are entangled.

And yet, above all that, there is definitely a common
European attitude toward the debts. And this we do not
easily comprehend. It is probably not what it seems, that
is to say, not a feeling against the debts for any reason
given, neither that nor a conviction of their spiritual
enormity, as the propagandists keep saying, but a deep
natural resentment at the sudden rise of the United States
to the position of dominant world power. This was bound
to have happened in any case; however, it did happen

during the war, and such is the association in the European mind. And this was a more significant event than the war itself. The war was nothing new for Europe except in magnitude. Those who were enemies then had been allies before, and these who were allies then had been enemies before. Only the scars would be new. But for the first time in the common history of Europe a non-European power intervened for reasons of its own to decide the issue of a European quarrel, not for conquest, not for anything material it wanted, but because it could not bear it any longer, and for such reasons besides, as to make the world safe for democracy, the seas safe for neutrals, to impose upon Europe a peace without victory. It gained none of these ends; it lost them at the peace table. Old World diplomacy defeated it. Nevertheless, its power had been revealed. World power had been for many centuries one of Europe's unchallenged attributes; then in the midst of a homicidal quarrel as to which European member should have it next, the power itself departed. It appeared on another continent, beyond the reach of conquest. The center of the political earth had shifted. And if, since the war, European diplomacy has employed all the resources of its wisdom and experience to discover and act upon the susceptibilities and weaknesses of this new power, for any advantage, that is only what we might have expected. The debts of course. What were the debts but a bitter reminder of Europe's lost attribute?

At any rate, all the principal debtor governments from the beginning, their reluctant settlements notwithstanding, have had but one thought about their obligations to the American Treasury. That has been how not to pay them and yet not repudiate them. There was a problem for Old World diplomacy. Repudiation would be very simple, and for all we could or would do about it, perfectly safe; but unfortunately at the same time very unwise, for two reasons. In the first place, to repudiate their war debts, as they discovered, would cost them access to the private American reservoir. They would be unable to borrow any more in Wall Street. In the second place, to repudiate them would set a dangerous precedent in the world. Both Great Britain and France have large foreign investments. Great Britain's investments in foreign countries are probably twenty billions of dollars. Therefore, for fear of setting a bad example to debtors, if for no other reasons, they could not afford to repudiate their debts. Only Germany could afford to do that.

So a debt policy was evolved and it has never for one moment changed. It is not the policy of Great Britain alone, nor the policy of France alone, nor of both together. It is a European policy. The aim of it is to get rid of these war debts to the American Treasury by a political stroke. Propaganda for cancellation was not the stroke. It was only the preparation. The stroke would be to commit the American Government to the proposition that its debtors should pay, and could pay, only provided they were paid reparations by Germany, so that if Germany should cease to pay them, as of course she would, they might cease to pay us.

The American Government has steadily insisted that so far as it is concerned, war debts and German reparations are unrelated. Nevertheless, Europe has stuck to her theme, trusting time, events and her skill of diplomacy to establish it.

THE END

COSIMO is an innovative publisher of books and publications that inspire, inform and engage readers worldwide. Our titles are drawn from a range of subjects including health, business, philosophy, history, science and sacred texts. We specialize in using print-on-demand technology (POD), making it possible to publish books for both general and specialized audiences and to keep books in print indefinitely. With POD technology new titles can reach their audiences faster and more efficiently than with traditional publishing.

> ➢ **Permanent Availability:** Our books & publications never go out-of-print.

> ➢ **Global Availability:** Our books are always available online at popular retailers and can be ordered from your favorite local bookstore.

COSIMO CLASSICS brings to life unique, rare, out-of-print classics representing subjects as diverse as *Alternative Health, Business and Economics, Eastern Philosophy, Personal Growth, Mythology, Philosophy, Sacred Texts, Science, Spirituality* and much more!

COSIMO-on-DEMAND publishes your books, publications and reports. If you are an Author, part of an Organization, or a Benefactor with a publishing project and would like to bring books back into print, publish new books fast and effectively, would like your publications, books, training guides, and conference reports to be made available to your members and wider audiences around the world, we can assist you with your publishing needs.

Visit our website at www.cosimobooks.com to learn more about Cosimo, browse our catalog, take part in surveys or campaigns, and sign-up for our newsletter.

And if you wish please drop us a line at info@cosimobooks.com. We look forward to hearing from you.

Printed in the United States
209053BV00001B/19-21/A

9 781596 056480